A Teen
Eating Disorder
Prevention
Book

Understanding
Compulsive
Eating

Carolyn Simpson

THE ROSEN PUBLISHING GROUP, INC.
NEW YORK

To Mom

Special thanks to Belinda Posey of Tulsa, Oklahoma, for her extensive research.

Published in 2000 by The Rosen Publishing Group, Inc.
29 East 21st Street, New York, NY 10010

First Edition

Cataloging-in-Publication Data

Simpson, Carolyn
    Understanding compulsive eating/ Carolyn Simpson.
        p. cm.— (A teen eating disorder prevention book)
    Includes bibliographical references and index.
    Summary: This book discusses compulsive eating, also called binge eating disorder, the factors that trigger this disorder, and treatment options that are available today.
    ISBN 0-8239-2989-2
    1. Compulsive eating— Juvenile literature. [1. Compulsive eating. 2. Eating disorders] I. Title. II. Series.
    616.85— dc21

Manufactured in the United States of America

ABOUT THE AUTHOR

Carolyn Simpson, a teacher and writer, has worked in the mental health field since 1973. She received a bachelor's degree in sociology from Colby College, Waterville, Maine, and a master's degree in Human Relations from the University of Oklahoma, Norman, Oklahoma.

She worked as a clinical social worker for ten years, both in Maine and Oklahoma, and as a teacher and counselor in the Young Parent's Program serving pregnant teens in Bridgton, Maine. Currently, she teaches psychology at Tulsa Community College in Tulsa, Oklahoma, and is an outpatient therapist at Parkside Behavioral Health Services in Tulsa.

She has written several other books in this series, including *Coping with Teenage Motherhood* and *Coping with Emotional Disorders*. She lives with her husband and their three children on the outskirts of Tulsa.

Contents

1. What Are Eating Disorders? 1

2. The Myth of the Ideal Body 15

3. Are You a Compulsive Eater? 23

4. Emotional Reasons for
   Compulsive Eating 37

5. Causes and Solutions 49

6. Do Diets Work? 63

7. Physiological Consequences of
   Compulsive Eating 68

8. Getting Professional Help 74

9. When a Friend Is a Compulsive
   Eater 85

10. Dealing with Compulsive Eating 91

    Glossary 111

    Where to Go for Help 114

    For Further Reading 118

    Index 121

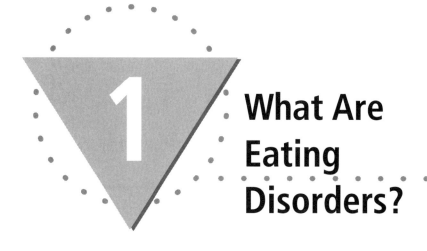

What Are Eating Disorders?

Food. You can't live without it. And to be healthy and happy, you need to know how to live with it.

Unfortunately, food has become a serious problem for millions of people in the United States. Many people have an unhealthy relationship with food. About 60 to 80 million Americans suffer from obesity. This means that they have an excess of body fat, which can cause serious health problems. Eight percent of Americans suffer from serious eating disorders. Because the social pressure on young women to be slim and model-like is particularly strong, more than 90 percent of those with eating disorders are teenage girls and young women.

Anyone can develop an eating disorder. Although it affects mostly white middle- to upper-class women, it can happen to males and females of all races, classes, and ages. It can happen to good students who are popular and successful adults who hold good jobs. But it can also happen to people who have problems, such as an addiction to drugs or alcohol, as well as to people who have been sexually abused or suffer from depression.

Athletes are vulnerable to eating disorders, particularly in those sports where weight is connected to performance. It can be a problem for dancers, weight lifters, wrestlers, gymnasts, swimmers, and long-distance runners. Males with eating disorders are often reluctant to get help. They may feel that an eating disorder is a "female problem," and they may be too embarrassed to seek help.

DISORDERED EATING

Disordered eating is not the same as an eating disorder such as bulimia, anorexia, or compulsive eating. In recent years, researchers studying eating disorders have discovered a wide variety of conditions, traits, and habits that can eventually lead to an eating disorder. This collection of behaviors is now known as disordered eating and is receiving more attention as the effort to prevent eating disorders has grown.

This new concept of disordered eating covers a wide range of abnormal eating behaviors. At one end are poor nutritional habits, which may include millions of people, and at the other end are true eating disorders such as anorexia and bulimia. This broadening of focus has allowed doctors, coaches, and counselors to recognize other seemingly less dangerous conditions that could lead to the extremes of anorexia or bulimia, and also to recognize that poor eating habits need not be as serious as persistent anorexia or bulimia. Experts estimate that an incredible 80 percent of all people are believed to be affected by borderline disordered eating, known technically as subclinical eating disorder. That means that only 20 percent of all people, or just one in five, have a healthy attitude toward food.

Dieting is the most common example of disordered eating. American society today is obsessed with thinness at any price, and the most common reaction to this overwhelming social pressure is to diet. At its simplest, the idea of dieting is to make a temporary change in one's eating habits to correct weight gain. When the proper weight is achieved, the diet stops.

There is a fundamental flaw in this concept, of course, which has been widely reported. Making a temporary change in one's eating habits to lose weight and then going back to eating "normally" will only lead to gaining weight again. The solution, promoted by nutritionists and doctors, is to make permanent changes in your eating habits so that your weight will stay at an ideal point. If you eat a good balance of healthy foods, consume the right number of calories, and exercise according to your individual needs, you shouldn't need to diet.

It sounds simple, but it's not. There is another hidden but very powerful factor involved—the battle between guilt and pleasure. The guilt stems from society's insistence that everyone should be model-thin. When a person doesn't measure up to this impossible ideal, he or she feels guilt and shame, and is likely to go on a diet. Dieting the old-fashioned, temporary way eases the conscience because it feels like penance. In the back of his or her mind, the dieter thinks, "If I suffer through this horrible diet and lose some weight, I will be acceptable." The other half of the equation, pleasure, is what prevents people from sticking to a permanent, healthy eating plan. Food tastes good, and eating can sometimes become a substitute for other, unsatisfied desires. And, of course, we are encouraged to eat.

Ironically, while society demands that we diet to be thin and therefore acceptable, it also bombards us with the message that we should indulge in every pleasurable activity that we can. Every commercial for a soft drink, a cereal, a candy bar, or a restaurant is based on this premise. Our appetites and taste buds have been conditioned to demand fatty, sugary foods, and we have been encouraged to eat and drink nutritionally poor processed foods containing artificial flavorings, and so we choose what to eat based on what tastes good, not on what nutrients we need for the day. With so many "luscious," "rich," and "sinfully delicious" foods to choose from, it's not hard to turn away from the healthy foods. When it comes to food, we are encouraged to indulge in the so-called guilty pleasures as often as we feel the urge, but we are also expected to abstain from rich foods from time to time and to diet so that we can be perfect. With such mixed messages, is it any wonder that so many Americans suffer from disordered eating?

Sometimes disordered eating gets completely out of control and turns into a full-fledged eating disorder, such as anorexia, bulimia, or BED (binge eating disorder). Each of these conditions has its own unique characteristics, but what they all have in common is that the sufferer has an unhealthy relationship with food.

ANOREXIA

Gina had been taking ballet lessons since she was five years old. Last summer, just before entering eighth grade, Gina suddenly grew four inches taller and began developing breasts and hips. She is now taller than her dance teacher and is two sizes larger than her mother. Her family and friends kid Gina, calling her Big Bird in school and at the dance academy.

But Gina doesn't want to stand out; she wants to fit in. She is so worried about the prospect of growing even bigger that she is uncomfortable eating. She has come up with a plan for losing the weight she has gained and preventing herself from growing any more.

Gina keeps a list of everything she eats during the week. The shorter the list, the better she feels about herself. Gina, who used to be a healthy eater, now has only three cups of non-fat yogurt and two bowls of cereal on her weekly list of food. She is proud of her ability to stick to her plan. She even enjoys feeling hungry, because to her it's proof of her determination and strong character.

Anorexia nervosa is often called anorexia for short. Anorexia nervosa literally means "loss of appetite," but this is a misleading definition. A person with anorexia nervosa is hungry, just like everyone else, but denies the hunger because of an irrational fear of becoming fat. Anorexia nervosa is often characterized by self-starvation, preoccupation with food, food rituals (eating only at certain times and in certain ways), compulsive exercising, and frequently an absence of menstrual cycles. Untreated, anorexia can be fatal. It is not a phase that the victim will outgrow if left alone, like purple hair, and parents must understand this. The most common cause of death in a long-time anorexic is low serum potassium, which can cause an irregular heartbeat.

There are numerous physical consequences for a person who suffers from anorexia. The most immediate effect is weight loss. At first, the drop in weight may not be noticeable or may not look particularly unhealthy. But in a short time the weight loss becomes dramatic and threatens the body's well-being. Anorexia affects all of the body's functions. As the disorder progresses, digestion slows down and you become constipated. You're always cold because you've lost the protective layer of fat that insulates you. Fine hair, called lanugo, grows all over your body. If you're a female, your menstrual period stops. You will also look and feel weak and tired, have a pasty complexion, lose your hair, and have fainting spells and headaches. The palms of your hands and the soles of your feet turn yellow because your body lacks many of the essential nutrients it needs to function properly.

When you aren't getting enough nutrition from your food, your body will start to break down muscles to produce energy. Your liver and kidneys are damaged from this stress, leading to kidney failure. This can be fatal, or require you to be on dialysis for the rest of your life. Anorexia may also make females infertile, as fertility depends on having a certain amount of body fat. You may also develop osteoporosis—a condition in which your bones become brittle and may even break. Your heart can be affected. Anorexia disturbs the mineral balance in your body, which can cause cardiac arrest and death.

Anorexia usually begins with a simple diet and progresses to an intense power struggle over weight and food. The person will also use eating as a way of controlling the people close to her. Self-denial makes her feel virtuous and powerful. Nothing gives her as much pleasure as dieting and losing weight, even when her health is suffering.

BULIMIA

Some days Ellie feels so out of control about her eating that she can't stop. Especially after a tough day, she finds herself bingeing on all the food she can find. She eats a whole bakery cake, a pound of cheese with crackers, and a loaf of bread with butter and jelly. Then she washes it down with a sixty-four-ounce bottle of diet soda. When she's done, she feels so nauseous that it's easy to make herself throw up. Then she feels drained but relieved that all those calories she has just eaten won't be able to make her fatter. She has kept this a secret for years. Not even her family knows what she is doing.

Bulimia nervosa is characterized by recurring periods of binge eating, during which large amounts of food are consumed in a short period of time—sometimes as much as 20,000 calories during the course of a single binge. Normally, a diet of 3,000 calories would be adequate for the entire day. The bulimic is aware that his or her eating is out of control. The bulimic is fearful of not being able to stop eating and is also afraid of being fat. Bulimia, like all eating disorders, can have devastating effects on the body. There are several common medical problems that people with bulimia can develop. If bulimia is left untreated, a person may need to be hospitalized. The longer the eating disorder remains untreated, the worse the problems become.

Since people who suffer from bulimia tend to be secretive about their behavior and do not exhibit the dramatic physical changes associated with severe weight loss or emaciation, how can you tell if a person is suffering from bulimia? Two organizations, Eating Disorders Awareness and Prevention, Inc., (EDAP) and Eating Disorders/Shared Awareness (EDSA), have both outlined specific warning signs that people with bulimia may exhibit.

In women, bulimia can cause an irregular menstrual cycle, or menstruation may even stop completely. New studies have found that the loss of the menstrual cycle, or amenorrhea, can cause other health problems as well. Women who don't get their periods lack sufficient estrogen, which helps to maintain strong bones. A lack of estrogen can cause osteoporosis, a disease that weakens the bones.

Dehydration from purging causes dry skin, brittle nails and hair, and loss of hair. Bleeding gums result from the lack of vitamins and minerals in the body. Purging rituals also take food out of the body before nutrients can be absorbed, causing malnutrition.

The pressure of repeated vomiting can cause the blood vessels in the eyes, face, and arms to break. It can also lead to puffiness and swelling in the hands, feet, and face. Because of enlarged salivary glands, people with bulimia usually have swollen cheeks. And in addition to causing fatigue, skin problems, and weak eyesight, vitamin and mineral deficiencies can also result in serious harm to the person's heart, kidneys, and bones.

The teeth develop cavities or ragged edges, and the gums may be swollen and tender from the strong stomach acids that are brought into the mouth from repeated vomiting. A person who frequently purges is likely to develop tooth decay and gum disease, and may possibly lose teeth. The bulimic may also have a very sore throat, severe stomach pains, cramps, and indigestion. In extreme cases of repeated purging, erosion of the esophagus and the lining of the stomach can occur. A hole in the esophagus can cause sudden death.

If someone purges frequently with laxatives, that person may become constipated or dependent on laxatives for normal bowel movements. Medications such as ipecac are especially dangerous. Ipecac is normally used by parents or physicians in an emergency to induce vomiting when someone accidentally swallows poison. However, if used improperly, ipecac can also be a poison. Ipecac stays in your cells. If a bulimic takes ipecac regularly for even a few weeks, that person can actually die from overuse of this medicine. People who have overused ipecac have died from congestive heart failure.

The most dangerous physical side effect of bulimia is an electrolyte imbalance. Electrolytes are electrically charged ions necessary for the proper functioning of all of the body's major systems. Repeated purging causes a depletion of the electrolytes potassium, chromium, and sodium. An electrolyte imbalance can cause kidney problems, muscle spasms, heart irregularities, and death.

A person who suffers from anorexia nervosa shares certain symptoms with a person who has bulimia nervosa. This is the reason why "nervosa" is part of both terms. In fact, about 50 percent of the people who have bulimia had anorexia first. In both cases, the person is preoccupied with dieting, food, weight, and body size. But there are also a few differences. People with anorexia deny to themselves and to others that there is a problem. They genuinely see themselves as overweight, even when it's obvious that they are dangerously underweight. But people with bulimia are aware that there is a problem, even though they may try to keep it a secret from others.

Formal diagnoses of anorexia and bulimia are made based on a set of criteria in the *Diagnostic and Statistical Manual of Mental Disorders* (DSM), a guidebook used by mental health professionals. In order to be considered anorexic, according to the DSM, a person must be at least 15 percent lighter than the minimum body weight for his or her height. To be diagnosed a bulimic, a person must average at least two binge-and-purge sessions per week for at least three months.

Ultimately, however, the two disorders have more similarities than differences. People with bulimia and anorexia always fear that they will get fat—no matter how thin they are. They feel that being thin means being happy. People with anorexia and bulimia have an inability to deal with uncomfortable feelings. They have a distorted body image, seeing their bodies as being much larger than they really are. As a result, they use dangerous methods to lose weight and refuse to eat in a healthy manner.

COMPULSIVE EXERCISE

Compulsive exercise is also considered a serious eating disorder–related problem. This disorder occurs when a person constantly exercises to get rid of calories.

Anabel finally realized that she might be obsessed with working out when her parents found her on the treadmill, trying to run with her leg in a cast. She had developed a stress fracture from running on the track team, and although it really hurt to put weight on it, she was determined to continue her rigorous exercise regimen. She was leaning on the bars and trying to run on the other leg.

What makes exercise "compulsive"? This question can be hard to answer. Most people find it hard to believe that when it comes to exercise, there can be too much of a good thing. In the case of a competitive athlete or sports enthusiast, compulsive exercise is easily disguised as healthy behavior. The compulsive exerciser looks like a motivated, committed athlete with a strong, admirable desire to be the best.

If you exercise regularly or participate in a sport, ask yourself why you do it. Is it because you enjoy the activity, because you like to win, or because you know that exercise is an important component of overall health? Or is there more to it than that? If you quit your team or skipped your workouts for a while, how would you feel about yourself? Would you feel guilty or worthless? "Signs of obsession include feelings of acute anxiety over a missed workout and an urge to make exercise a priority over friends and family," Alicia Potter noted in an article for the *Boston Phoenix*. "Most trainers recommend working out no more than an hour a day." Another warning sign, according to Anorexia Nervosa and Related Eating Disorders, Inc., (ANRED), is "when the activity ceases being fun and becomes a duty, a chore, an obligation that is definitely not fun, but that you must do—or else suffer strong guilt or anxiety."

If your self-esteem is based largely on your performance in a sport or in your ability to stick to a workout regimen, or if your training program consumes hours every day, gets in the way of relationships with friends and family, interferes with school or work, or involves dangerous tactics such as steroid use, you may be headed for a problem with exercise compulsion.

COMPULSIVE EATING

There is a fourth and more common food-related problem called compulsive eating, also known as binge eating disorder (BED). Compulsive eating is similar to bulimia in that the person is unable to keep from consuming large amounts of food at one time, but unlike bulimia, the person usually does not purge the food. Therefore, most people suffering from compulsive eating are often overweight or obese. An estimated 30 percent of people participating in medically supervised weight control programs are found to be suffering from compulsive eating, compared to an average of 2 percent of the population overall.

As with anorexia and bulimia, compulsive eating is more common among women than men—approximately 60 percent of its victims are female—but men make up a much larger percentage of compulsive-eating sufferers than they do for any other eating disorder. Compulsive eaters feel overwhelming shame at being unable to control their eating and are also likely to have low self-esteem or even suffer from depression. It is important to recognize that the inability to keep from overeating is not just gluttony or laziness. It is a disease, and its sufferers, like those of any other disease, need help to overcome it.

If you think you may be a compulsive eater or in danger of becoming one, or if you know someone who is struggling with overeating, this book will help you to understand the problem better and to find help in dealing with this disorder. It is important to know that this is not a diet book. Nor does it offer quick and easy cures. However, it does discuss some of the cultural, social, and personal factors that can trigger compulsive eating, and it provides guidance for teens who want to find long-term solutions to this painful problem.

The Myth of the Ideal Body

Ask a group of people to describe the ideal body and you'll probably hear a variety of answers. Someone will cite the name of a famous model or celebrity, or maybe a set of measurements, or a description of the size and shape of certain body parts. One answer you will surely never hear, not even from models and movie stars, is, "The ideal body is my body."

Nearly everyone who believes that there is an ideal body describes it as thinner, stronger, healthier, better, or in some other way different from his or her own body. The ideal body is always something that we lack, something that we can never achieve—not with diets, pills, or even plastic surgery. In other words, the ideal body is always impossible to attain because we can never allow ourselves to believe that our own bodies are good enough.

CULTURAL IDEAS ABOUT BEING FAT AND BEING THIN

Do you sometimes wake up in the morning, look in

15

the mirror, and say, "I feel fat today." But how can you feel fat? Fat is not a feeling, like happiness, sadness, excitement, or fear. When you say "I feel fat," you are not really talking about the size of your body. Instead, you are telling yourself, "I'm not good enough."

Maybe you are nervous about a test at school or afraid that nobody will ask you to the school dance. Maybe you feel like an outsider with your classmates or you are having problems with your parents. These situations can be difficult to deal with, and you may find it easier to blame your body for all of your bad feelings. Maybe you believe that all your problems would disappear if you were thinner.

It is easy to see why people become dissatisfied with their bodies when they experience problems. We live in a culture that teaches us that we should never be happy with the size and shape of our bodies. Everywhere we look—in the movies, on television, in magazines and newspapers, on billboards and other advertisements—we get the message that fat is bad and unhealthy, and thin is beautiful and healthy.

The fashion sections of magazines for girls and women show ultrathin models wearing the latest styles, leading most teens to think that their own bodies are not good enough. Then the health and fitness sections of the same magazines seem to offer help by promising a thinner, smaller body after just a few weeks on some fad diet. But the slim shapes featured in magazines are impossible for most of us to achieve. People come in a variety of shapes and sizes, and each type of body has its own beauty. It's easy to forget that the slim figures featured in magazines are just one of many different body shapes.

Although being slim is in fashion today, that hasn't always been the case. In past centuries, a full, fleshy body was considered desirable because it signified wealth, beauty, and fertility. Paintings by the great seventeenth-century masters of Western art, Rembrandt and Rubens, featured big, beautiful women. Curves were popular on female figures until a few decades ago, and in the 1950s and early 1960s, a full-figured Marilyn Monroe was America's most celebrated sex symbol. It is only in the last twenty or thirty years that our nation's obsession with being thin has become so intense and widespread.

THE CHANGING ROLES OF MEN AND WOMEN

Although both men and women may suffer from a poor self-image as a result of weight problems, the issue is particularly difficult for girls because the female body naturally has a higher percentage of body fat than the male body. As they grow older, girls develop a protective layer of fat on their breasts, tummies, and hips in preparation for their child-bearing years, and boys' bodies grow firmer and more muscular.

These differences are healthy and natural. But the changing roles of men and women in our society have helped to create an unhealthy myth of the ideal body. Women have advanced in traditionally male areas of life, such as business and sports. But some critics argue that people have come to expect that women's bodies should be more like men's—hard, strong, and muscular—in order for women to perform as well as men in these areas. Such demands are unhealthy and often impossible.

PEER PRESSURE

The myth of the ideal body can be particularly troubling for teens because the teenage years are full of difficult physical and emotional changes. Puberty can be especially difficult for girls because their bodies naturally put on more weight to prepare for menstruation. Many teens think that they will not be popular if they have the wrong body shape. But most are unaware that genetics play a big part in determining their body shapes.

Teens with bodies that don't fit the current ideal of beauty often fear that they will never be sexually attractive to anyone. Well-meaning friends and family members sometimes make these insecurities worse by suggesting dangerous solutions, such as fad diets and diet pills. The real solution is for teens to learn to love and accept themselves—no matter what their body size or shape—and find healthier ways to deal with food and feelings.

GENETICS AND BODY SHAPE

When girls and boys grow into women and men, why do so many people suddenly expect their bodies to have a "right" size and shape unrelated to family traits? Doesn't it make sense that your bone structure and metabolic rate (the speed at which your body uses food for energy) are influenced by heredity as much as the curl of your hair and the color of your eyes?

It does make sense, and medical research has confirmed that it's true. Heredity matters more than diet, exercise, or any other single factor in determining the shape and size of our bodies. Scientists who studied a group of adopted babies throughout their lives found that in terms of size and weight, they were more like their birth parents than their adoptive parents. Similar results were found for sets of identical twins who were separated and raised in different families. With nothing in common except their genes, they grew up with virtually identical weights and body types. So it's not entirely true that you are what you eat.

If everyone in your family for the past three generations has been under six feet tall, no amount of exercise or special food is likely to make you grow taller than six feet. The same is true for many other physical features that you inherit from your parents, including your general body type. In today's world, it seems that we can change so much about ourselves, but when we work against our basic heredity, we are likely to be disappointed.

ALL BODIES NEED FUEL

Your body's work is going on constantly, renewing and replacing your billions of cells, whether you are running, sitting, lying down, or sleeping. Your most important muscle, your heart, is working every minute of your life. Dozens of muscles in your body are contracting and stretching all the time so that you can breathe, blink, yawn, swallow, or just think.

All of this activity requires energy, which comes from food. We require many different kinds of nutrients, but we get most of our energy for daily living from carbohydrates, foods made up of starches and complex sugars. Examples of foods that are high in carbohydrates are breads, cereals, pastas, and potatoes. In order to stay healthy and have enough energy to function, every person must take in about 3,000 calories every day. If you consume more than you need, the body is able to convert the extra calories into fat and store it in body tissues.

STORED ENERGY

When the foods you eat provide less energy, which we measure in calories, than you use in a day, your body doesn't refuse to work. If it did, you would stop breathing. Instead, it unlocks stored energy deposited throughout your body on the days when you ate more calories than you needed. The stored calories are available from the fat and muscle tissue in your body.

Every body maintains a fat supply as its first source of stored energy. This is one of the many reasons why a certain amount of body fat is essential to good health. Your fat also helps to maintain a proper body temperature and to cushion your bones. When a woman's fat supply falls far below healthy levels, her body stops producing estrogen. Menstruation can stop completely. Every person has a certain amount of natural body fat and a unique rate of metabolism. To try to alter your natural levels of fat or your metabolism as you

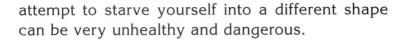
attempt to starve yourself into a different shape can be very unhealthy and dangerous.

EATING HAS GOTTEN EASIER

Food is necessary for human life. We need a balanced diet to fuel our bodies and maintain nutritional health. Our ancestors had to grow or kill their own food to survive, and their diets were simple. Sometimes there wasn't enough food, and people got sick and died. Today most of us can go to a grocery store or a restaurant and buy whatever we want to eat. At fast-food restaurants, we can get food without even leaving the car. Pizza parlors and Chinese restaurants deliver to our homes. Food is readily available, plentiful, and convenient, and we can pick what we want from foods grown and manufactured all over the world. Of course, fast foods and convenience foods are designed for quick and easy preparation and long shelf life, not necessarily for good nutrition, and they often have a high sugar or fat content and are mixed with various food additives and flavorings.

THE CONTRADICTION

One of the results of having all this convenience food is that much of the food we eat is unhealthy for us, and it has become harder to eat a balanced diet. Yet we are a culture obsessed with health and fitness, so that millions of us are struggling with what and how much we eat. Many people have developed a love/hate relationship with food. Our feelings about food have become a national problem because we have become obsessed with our physical appearance and the unattainable goal of having perfect bodies. Between the desires of the food industry to make us loyal and gluttonous consumers of their products, and the desires of the fashion, cosmetic, and exercise industries to mold us all into perfect imitations of movie stars, many people are caught in an endless struggle to control their weight and size. They suffer severe emotional problems when they can't achieve the impossible, and these feelings only make it more difficult to control their intake of food.

Are You a Compulsive Eater?

Most people overeat now and then, and that's normal. But if you often eat until you are overstuffed, or if you eat large amounts of food when you are not really hungry or it's not a regular mealtime, you may be a compulsive eater. A compulsive-eating disorder left untreated can lead to serious health problems, such as high blood pressure, heart disease, and diabetes, as well as psychological problems. It is important to determine as early as possible whether there is a problem. The earlier it is identified, the sooner the problem can be treated.

DO I HAVE A PROBLEM?

You may be a compulsive eater if you:

- ⊙ Never stop thinking about food

- ⊙ Have trouble recognizing when your body is really hungry and usually eat well beyond the point of fullness

⊙ Eat large amounts of food, often in a short period of time, and always finish everything, whether you're hungry or not

⊙ Use food to avoid doing things that you don't want to do, to manage stressful situations, and to comfort yourself when you're feeling sad, angry, lonely, bored, nervous, or scared

⊙ Prefer to eat alone, or you hide food and eat it secretly

⊙ Go on and off diets, repeatedly losing and gaining back large amounts of weight

⊙ Feel out of control when you eat

⊙ Judge yourself as good or bad according to what foods you eat and what size you are

⊙ Feel ashamed of or disgusted by your body and your eating habits

⊙ Think of eating as one of your only pleasures in life, yet feel guilty about it

A person who compulsively eats struggles with food because he or she has developed patterns of food abuse similar to the patterns of an alcoholic abusing alcohol or a drug addict abusing drugs. For the compulsive eater, these patterns seem impossible to break because his or her eating habits are usually established during childhood.

TYPES OF COMPULSIVE EATING

The three common patterns of compulsive eating are secretive snacking, grazing, and binge eating. Some compulsive eaters may have all of these eating habits; others may have just one or two.

Secretive Snacking

When Kathy was thirteen, she started at a new junior high school. None of her old school friends were there to support her. She often found herself sitting alone at a corner table during lunch period. This made her so uncomfortable that she sometimes skipped lunch and hid in the girls' room until the bell rang.

Kathy had been a bit overweight as a child. As a teenager she noticed that she had grown larger than most of the other girls in her class. She felt ashamed of her body. She started to wear big sweaters and to make excuses so she wouldn't have to change for gym class.

Kathy's mother, who had been thin and popular as a child, thought that if Kathy lost weight she might be able to make friends and gain some confidence. She found a diet in a magazine and showed it to Kathy.

At first, Kathy was very excited about dieting. After a few weeks, she started to lose some weight. However, her situation at school did not change. She still felt lonely, and she didn't want to sit with anyone in the cafeteria while she ate diet food. Worst of all, Kathy was hungry all the time, but she was reluctant to ask her mother for more food because she didn't want to disappoint her.

Late one night, Kathy got out of bed to use the bathroom. Her stomach was growling. She tiptoed downstairs and ate a leftover chicken leg that she found in the refrigerator. She felt better immediately. She went back to bed and slept through the night. After that, Kathy started sneaking food whenever her mother wasn't looking. She'd get up and fix herself peanut butter sandwiches after everyone had gone to bed, or she'd sneak into the kitchen in the middle of the day and eat just a little bit of all the leftovers in the refrigerator so that nobody would notice the missing food.

Soon Kathy's mother started to ask her why she was gaining back weight. She talked about Kathy's weight all the time and reduced Kathy's meals with the family to smaller and smaller portions. The more Kathy's mother crit-icized her daughter's weight problem, the more Kathy enjoyed sneaking snacks behind her mother's back.

Kathy is a compulsive eater who uses secretive snacking—eating snacks secretly, often late at night—as her main pattern of food abuse. Kathy feels hungry all the time because of her strict diet, but she also feels too guilty and ashamed to let oth-ers see her eating more food. She eats secretly because she doesn't want her mother to know that she is breaking her diet, but eating secretly also makes her feel powerful. Kathy is angry at her mother for making her follow a strict diet, but she is also afraid that her mother's love depends on whether she is fat or thin. Kathy can't express her anger directly, so she gets back at her mother by disobeying her.

Grazing

Craig, fourteen, was always bigger than the rest of the students in his class. As a little kid, he had been the last boy to be chosen for teams in gym class. And the team that got him would complain about his lack of coordination and skill. When Craig got to high school, though, the football coach noticed his large build and suggested that he join the school team.

At first Craig told the coach that he wasn't very good at sports, but the coach said that the team needed offensive linemen who, like Craig, were big, solid, and powerful. The coach also explained that weight training would help Craig build up his strength.

Craig was convinced. He thought that football might be a good way for him to make more friends and to show that he could be good at sports. He spent the summer before his sophomore year eating more than ever, drinking power shakes, studying videos about football, and lifting weights at the local YMCA. His weight ballooned up to nearly 230 pounds.

When Craig showed up for football training in August, all the guys on the team were amazed to see how much he had bulked up. He was bigger than ever and looked powerful. He joined the team and played successfully. Craig was so big and strong and such a big eater that he soon earned the nickname Ox. At lunch, kids would sit at his table and make bets on how much he could eat.

Craig soon found himself eating constantly—snacking on candy bars between classes, munching cookies in the locker room before and after practice, eating at home in front of the open refrigerator door while talking to friends on the phone. Craig's mother worried about her son's weight gain, but Craig's father told her that she shouldn't be concerned because their son was a football star.

By the end of his sophomore year, Craig weighed nearly 270 pounds. Because of his elevated blood pressure and high cholesterol count, the coach told him he wouldn't be able to play football again in the fall.

Craig is a compulsive eater who uses grazing—overeating at different times and places throughout the day—as his main pattern of food abuse. Unlike Kathy, Craig does not appear to be ashamed of overeating because he does it in front of people. But inside, he does not feel good about what he does. He suffers from low self-esteem, and he uses food to gain attention and acceptance instead of letting people get to know the real person inside the body.

Binge Eating

Anna, fifteen, was a bright girl with many friends. She had a great sense of humor and was always joking around and making people laugh. Anna was overweight, but none of her friends ever mentioned it to her because it never seemed important.

However, Anna had a secret. Her home life was not happy. Anna was an only child. Her mother had died when she was ten, and she lived alone with her father. Anna's father sometimes drank too much, and when he was drunk he often became violent. He said cruel things to Anna and even threatened to hit her.

Whenever this happened, Anna would run upstairs, lock herself in her room, and turn up the television really loud. Then she would take out the supply of candy, cookies, cakes, and potato chips that she kept hidden under her bed and on the top shelf in her closet. While her father yelled and threw things downstairs, Anna would open two or three large bags of potato chips and eat all of them without stopping. Sometimes she would devour three or four packages of chocolate-chip cookies or several boxes of cupcakes. As Anna ate, she would stop feeling afraid about what her father was doing downstairs. All she would think about was eating.

Anna would eat like this for one or two hours, depending on how much her father had upset her. When she finished, she usually felt tired and disappointed. She would hide all of the empty bags, boxes, and wrappers under her bed, turn off the light, and try to sleep. However, Anna usually had trouble falling asleep. She would begin to talk to herself. She'd tell herself that she was fat, ugly, disgusting, and out of control, and she would often end up crying herself to sleep.

The next day, Anna would go down to breakfast, and she and her father would both pretend that nothing bad had happened the previous night. Anna would go to school, tell jokes, and make her friends laugh, and everyone would think that everything was normal.

Anna is a compulsive eater who uses binge eating—eating unusually large amounts of food in a short period of time—as her main pattern of food abuse. Anna binges as a reaction to her father's alcoholism. Because she can't talk about her problems with her friends or deal with her father's drinking, Anna uses bingeing as a way to escape the fear and anger she feels when her father loses control. The relief that she feels while bingeing is only temporary. Anna always ends up criticizing and blaming herself. And, unfortunately, when she stops eating, her situation at home is still the same.

COMPULSIVE EATING AND BULIMIA

According to the dictionary, a compulsion is "an irresistible impulse to act, regardless of the rationality of the motivation." Compulsive behavior is automatic—people put themselves on autopilot when they don't know how to deal with their feelings.

Compulsive eating, like other types of compulsive behavior, involves doing things that you realize are harmful, even though you can't stop. You find yourself thinking about food all the time—either how to get it or how to avoid it. Because you are unable to control yourself around certain foods, you are a compulsive eater. Bulimics share many behavior patterns with compulsive eaters, in the sense that they often feel out of control and compelled to binge on huge amounts of food.

Although a clinical distinction is made between bulimics and compulsive eaters, in reality the two disorders may be very hard to tell apart. Many compulsive eaters purge the food they eat, but they do not do it frequently enough to be considered bulimics. Compulsive eaters may even find that they binge with the intention of throwing up afterward, and then find they cannot bring themselves to induce the vomiting.

Sharon's English teacher was handing back exams. Sharon knew that she hadn't done well. When the teacher looked at the floor as she handed Sharon her exam, Sharon knew it was bad. Her stomach started to churn.

Sharon stole a quick glance at the red numbers in the upper right corner—66. She hid her paper in her notebook. She was feeling weak, and all she could think about was food. She was supposed to go over to her friend Jana's house after school and work on their project for Spanish class, but she knew she wouldn't do that. Maybe later she could think about the project. Right now, all she could think about was eating cookie-dough ice cream.

Sharon failed to meet her friend that afternoon and went alone to the grocery store. She grabbed a shopping basket and headed directly toward the freezer section. On the way, she spotted a guy from her English class.

"I can't let him see me buying ice cream,"

she thought. So she headed to the salad bar and made herself a large vegetable and lettuce salad instead. Then she bought a box of crackers to go with the salad. But she still wasn't ready to head for the checkout line. She kept thinking about that half gallon of ice cream. She turned back toward the freezer section. On the way, she passed the cookie aisle and piled a few packages of cookies into the basket. Then she found her ice cream and placed a carton of cookie dough and a carton of caramel fudge (because she couldn't decide between the two) into her basket. At last, she made her way to the checkout counter.

Once she had paid for the food, she hurried out to the car. As soon as she got home, she piled all the food on the counter. Her mother would be home in an hour, so she had to eat fast.

She started with the salad. The salad could have fed three people, but Sharon ate it all herself. Then she ate the whole box of crackers. She scooped out half the carton of cookie-dough ice cream and half the caramel fudge into a serving dish. She ate the ice cream, then moved on to the cookies. At first she felt dreamy and contented as she ate, but then her stomach started to feel as if it would burst. Sharon looked at the clock. Her mother would be home in twenty minutes. She couldn't leave any evidence. She had to eat everything. No matter how stuffed she felt, she had to finish it all. As she ate, she promised herself that she'd throw it all up afterward. It would be as if nothing had ever happened.

At last she finished the ice cream, cookies, crackers, and salad. She threw the empty cartons in the trash, tied up the trash bag, and brought it to the trash can. Then she put a new liner in the kitchen waste basket and headed for the bathroom. She lifted the toilet lid and stared into the bowl. This was the moment of truth. She began to shake. All the food in her stomach seemed to turn into a rock. She felt nauseous and disgusted with herself, but somehow she just couldn't throw up. She tried sticking her fingers down her throat, but after a few tries she sat back with tears streaming down her face. "I can't even do this right," she thought to herself.

Exhausted, she took off her clothes and climbed into the tub to soak and rest. She was too tired to feel the anxiety she'd felt earlier about her low grade. Besides, all she could feel now was the guilt from spending money and eating all that food. She hadn't really enjoyed any of it, and worse, she hadn't been able to control herself at all. She hated herself when she did this.

"I won't do this ever again," she told herself. "In fact, I'll skip dinner."

Of the 60 to 70 million people who are compulsive eaters, 85 percent are women. Not all of them binge by eating huge amounts at a sitting. Some people just eat consistently throughout the day.

Compulsive eaters usually do not purge afterward. If they overeat and don't fast or diet, they ultimately become overweight. Some 22 percent of children in the United States are obese, weighing 30 percent more than their ideal body weight. But people's eating behavior can vary greatly.

For example, some people eat fast and furiously. As you will see later, this behavior is usually learned from watching others. After a while, they become accustomed to the overstuffed feeling and associate it with any meal. Some compulsive overeaters nibble instead of binge. They spread their eating out over the day or night. They will never eat a whole box of cookies or a family-size bag of chips in one sitting, but they will eat both over the space of a few hours.

Sometimes compulsive eating starts with dieting. This can start the cycle of starving and bingeing. People stick to a rigid diet all day long, particularly when they're around other people, and eat late at night or when they're alone. Then they binge on all the food they denied themselves during the past days or week.

Some compulsive eaters started out as plate cleaners. They are simply obedient children who learned at an early age to eat everything on their plates. They had to keep eating, even when their stomachs told them that they were full, because they were told that it was sinful to waste food. After a while, many plate cleaners simply eat everything in front of them without asking themselves whether they're hungry or stuffed.

Finally, some compulsive eaters are comfort eaters. They eat normal amounts of food most of the time, except when they are stressed. Then they turn to food to make themselves feel better, either by bingeing or perpetually nibbling.

Most compulsive eaters either wage a constant

war with their weight by dieting, or they allow themselves to become overweight. Even if they have managed to maintain a relatively average weight, they know they have an unhealthy relationship with food. People who are overweight also face pressure from a society that is obsessed with thinness. They live lives of continual disappointment, depression, and low self-esteem because their appetites betray their desires to look the way others think they should look.

Much in the same way that alcoholics are addicted to alcohol, compulsive eaters are addicted to, or hooked on, food. Their lives are controlled by thoughts of what, when, and how much they will eat. As a result, many compulsive eaters are also addicted to dieting. They believe that diets can help them to control their obsession with food. Typically, they become yo-yo dieters, constantly losing and regaining weight in an unhealthy way.

Compulsive eaters are not alone in thinking of themselves as good when they are eating low-fat foods and losing weight and as bad when they are eating fattening foods and gaining weight. Many people feel guilty about what they eat, but those who eat compulsively take these feelings to an extreme. They feel so guilty about their lack of self-control that they often eat alone or hide their food and eat it secretly. They eat whether or not they are hungry. They often consume large amounts of sweets and high-calorie foods and do not stop until they feel uncomfortably full. Compulsive eaters usually feel ashamed of their bodies and judge themselves and the way they eat in a harsh and unkind manner.

Most teenage girls and many teenage boys have probably experienced some of the problems described in this chapter. It is nearly impossible to live in a culture obsessed with fitness and thinness without having a negative body image at least some of the time. However, teens who suffer from compulsive eating are never free of these bad feelings.

No matter how smart, talented, or decent they are, compulsive eaters feel that their problems with food and weight make them unworthy of the fun, friendship, and happiness that other teens share. They struggle to fill an empty space in their lives with food, but the hunger inside can never be satisfied unless they start to change the way that they think about themselves, the feelings that prompt them to overeat, and the amounts and types of food they eat.

4 Emotional Reasons for Compulsive Eating

Experts note that there are two types of hunger: physical and emotional. Physical hunger is the slight discomfort or gnawing feeling you get in your stomach when it is empty and in need of food. This is a normal and healthy signal that lets you know when it's time to eat. Emotional hunger, on the other hand, has little to do with the body's physical needs. When people experience emotional hunger, they eat to try to fill an emptiness they feel in their hearts and minds.

Because compulsive eaters have learned to eat in response to their emotional needs instead of their physical needs, they often reach a point at which they are no longer able to experience and recognize real hunger. With the messages between the brain and the stomach short-circuited, compulsive eaters continue to think that they are hungry even after eating too much. Overeating often leads to weight gain, and weight gain usually leads to more of the same painful feelings that caused the person to turn to food in the first place.

Joey was the younger of two brothers. He was also the heavier of the two boys and seemed to be the one with all the bad luck. Both brothers were on the school football team. His brother, Lucas, was the gifted wide receiver, but Joey was a second-string lineman who only played when their team was leading by twenty-four points or more.

Lucas was planning to go to college on a football scholarship. Joey had neither the grades nor the athletic skill to win a scholarship. That made him angry a lot of the time. Whenever Lucas had an exceptionally good day on the field, Joey found himself at the neighborhood deli after the game. He ordered sandwiches, coleslaw, potato salad, and baked beans, and ate everything in silence. Sometimes he sat with his second-string teammates.

"Hey, man," a teammate would say. "Are you really going to eat all that?"

"Sure," Joey would say, hesitating with the fork to his mouth. "I didn't eat much for breakfast."

"Well, Lucas must have eaten his Wheaties. He sure had a good game, huh?"

"He always has a good game," Joey muttered as he scooped up more potato salad. "Hey, are you going to finish that sandwich? I'll eat it if you're just going to let it go to waste."

Joey finished everything on his plate. He felt stuffed, as he always did after a game, but that was the whole point. Feeling stuffed, he went home and watched television for the rest of the night. What's more, he didn't have to feel that awful rage he felt when Lucas was once again the best man on the field.

EATING IN RESPONSE TO CONFLICT AND EMOTION

People eat for different reasons. Ideally, we should eat only because we are hungry and need physical nourishment. However, people also eat for emotional nourishment or when certain feelings make them uncomfortable.

Conflict is one common trigger of discomfort. Conflict can make you feel anxious, depressed, or angry, and it can lead to overeating. Interpersonal conflict flares up between two people or groups of people—for example, if you are fighting with your sister over who gets to use the car. Intrapersonal conflict, on the other hand, results from a conflict within yourself. If, for example, you behave in ways that don't fit your idealized picture of yourself, you feel guilt. Then food becomes a means for you to distract and calm yourself. Unfortunately, eating does not resolve the conflict. Instead, you wind up feeling powerless, and you may turn to food again.

Compulsive eaters also turn to food to deal with anxiety, depression, boredom, anger, and fear. And there is an odd correlation between the foods compulsive eaters will choose and their moods. If you are feeling unhappy or deprived, you may crave sweets. The more nurturing or reassurance you need, the more likely that you will turn to soft, creamy foods like ice cream or puddings. If you are angry, you may prefer snacks you have to crunch and chew hard, like nuts. If you are anxious, you may simply want to keep popping things in your mouth, like chips.

You may eat in response to happiness, too, because you think you don't deserve to be happy. Unconsciously, you may know that overeating brings pain and embarrassment. Eating compulsively when things are going well, then, reinforces low self-esteem.

EMOTIONAL HUNGER

Because eating is often a response to emotion, it's common for compulsive eaters to substitute physical hunger for emotional hunger. They are looking for emotional support and approval through food rather than from other human relationships, which have proved disappointing to them in the past.

Many people overcompensate for the emotional hunger they experienced in childhood. Many parents reward or punish their children by giving or withholding food. It is not that they attempt to starve children who are disobedient, but a special treat might be offered to a child who measures up to parents' expectations, whereas no such treat is offered to the child who is defiant. In the child's mind, there is a direct connection between food and parental love and approval. As young adults, these people will eat, not out of hunger, but to compensate for the absence of affection or emotional support in their lives.

DEALING WITH ABUSE

Sometimes people turn to food to calm themselves

after emotional, physical, or sexual abuse. In cases like this, food serves more than one purpose. Food is comforting, but it is also a distancing device. Girls who are continually abused may unconsciously overeat to gain weight, believing that if they make themselves unattractive, the abuse (especially if it's sexual) will stop. Some girls use this same tactic when trying to keep boyfriends at arms' length. If they are perceived as unattractive, maybe they won't be pushed into sexual activity they don't feel ready for.

Compulsive eating is also a way to punish yourself. Although it is comforting in the short term, it makes people feel bad in the long term. If people gain weight, they reason that they have been bad and deserve to suffer the consequences.

Therapists have long suspected a link between bingeing-and-purging behavior and sexual abuse. Victims of sexual abuse may go on eating binges to numb their feelings of horror at what they've been through or are still enduring. The purging then serves a dual purpose—to get rid of the calories and to get rid of the images of the abuse. The victim is vomiting up her "experience of ugliness." One of my patients once told me that she felt better only when she had made herself vomit. She would go through repeated cycles of bingeing and purging to wear herself out and obliterate the image of her abuser.

Many people who feel that they have no control over their lives, especially if they are being abused, try to take control of their eating. It is important to address the bulimic's need to control her food intake and stop purging, but it also is necessary to address the feelings that might be prompting her to eat compulsively.

EATING IS LEARNED BEHAVIOR

Children learn how to behave in large part by watching the adults around them. Children observe more of what people do more than what people say, and they imitate what they see. For some children, that means learning unhealthy eating patterns.

Roger came from a large family. Whenever the eight of them sat down at the dinner table, it turned into a war zone. Concerned about getting their share, both the kids and the adults overindulged. Knowing they wouldn't get another chance, they would take two helpings of everything. George would lean over his sister's plate to grab some dinner rolls and stash a couple of extras in his lap. Gina would fill her plate with vegetables, salad, and chicken, even though she didn't like all the things she took. Even Roger's mother worried that her family wouldn't leave her much, so she sampled most of the meal beforehand. The family often finished dinner in ten minutes and then left the table in a daze. They never talked to each other except to say "Hand me the chicken" or "Send the green beans this way."

Not surprisingly, all of the kids had trouble eating at their friends' houses because they were never able to wait for people to pass them food. Roger usually brought his lunch to school because it was hard for him to stand in line and wait while others chose their food. He would have had to fight down the urge to take the biggest pieces of turkey or the cookie with the most chocolate chips. "It's not that I'm even hungry for all that," Roger once explained to a counselor. "It's just that I feel that if I don't get a pile of food when it's first offered, I'll never get another chance."

Roger learned to eat voraciously because everyone else in his family did. Anyone who ate his meal in a leisurely fashion found that the serving dishes emptied before he got to sample any. People were in such a hurry to "get their fair share" that they never realized they were overeating at every meal. As a result, they learned to eat fast, barely chewing their food, and then associated that stuffed-to-the-gills feeling with every meal.

People who eat voraciously have usually learned this behavior. In some cases, children are merely copying the way their parents eat, even if current circumstances don't justify their hurried style. Parents brought up in poverty may eat more than they need to eat because of the desire to "never go hungry again." When they have children, their children watch how much or how fast their parents eat, and they learn it as normal behavior. Some children eat as if they are afraid of going hungry, even when that isn't the case. They have merely learned to eat the way their parents eat.

It's a hard pattern to change, even once children leave home. Although their parents won't follow them around to make sure they eat everything on their plates, children internalize these values and learn to disregard the signals that tell them they're full. If there is food still in front of them, it's meant to be eaten, especially if it has already been paid for.

And just as food can serve as a reward for doing well, it can serve as a consolation prize for losing. Some children learn to eat when they have lost because that's how their parents consoled them when they experienced a disappointment of some kind. Patterns of behavior are difficult to change, even when they are self-destructive patterns. Using food as a reward or a consolation prize sets children up to become emotional eaters later on.

POWER STRUGGLES

Food is often not an end in itself but a means to an end. People have been known to use food as a weapon against each other.

Millie is a slim, attractive woman who has a beautiful, but heavier, adolescent daughter. Millie has been fighting with her daughter for years. Although they disagree about a lot of things, their fights always erupt over food. Millie prepares low-calorie meals because she worries about Rose's "weight problem," but Rose dislikes the low-calorie food and buys fast-food hamburgers to supplement her mother's meals. Rose also likes candy and sweets.

It's a constant battle. Millie threatens Rose, saying things like "If you keep eating like this, I won't spend any more money on new clothes for you!" She occasionally bribes Rose, promising, "If you lose five pounds by the end of the month, I'll let you have a sleepover." Rose pretends to accommodate her mother, but she keeps eating as she pleases.

Millie has announced to her neighbors that she and Rose are going on a new diet. Rose frowns. "I'm not on the diet anymore, but Mom's doing great. I think she's losing weight for both of us," she says. "I know Mom wants me to look like a model, but I don't care if I do. That's Mom's hang-up. I'm okay the way I am."

It sounds as if Rose is genuinely happy with herself, and that the struggle is only her mother's problem. This may be partly true. But Rose also has learned that eating and gaining weight upset her mother. She has learned that although she doesn't have a lot of control over some parts of her life, she can control what she eats and how she looks, which ultimately affects her mother. Rose is struggling to assert herself, and she is using food as one way to do it.

EATING AS A SIGN OF LOVE

One of the lessons Veronica learned growing up was that food is associated with love. In her family, if her mother wanted to show someone affection, she made a nice meal, cooked a favorite dessert, or took that person out to dinner. Early in Veronica's marriage, her husband complained that she rarely said "I love you."

"What do you mean?" she exclaimed. "I

say it all the time. Don't you remember that lasagna I made you the other night? I made that from scratch. And what about the choco-late cheesecake? That took me hours to make."

"What's food got to do with love?" her husband asked.

"It shows I love you," she said, exasperated that he had to ask. "I made your favorite meal. Doesn't that tell you anything?"

"Well, how was I supposed to know what that meant?" he asked.

"Well, I always cook you your favorite desserts after a fight," she replied.

"You mean you say you're sorry with food, too?" he asked.

"Of course," said Veronica. "In my family, you say you're sorry with food, you say you're glad to see someone with food, you say you love someone by giving them food."

"It must be hard not to be overweight in your family," her husband said, smiling.

Even though the use of food to say "I love you" or "I'm sorry" may seem harmless enough, some-times children come to associate parental love with the pleasures of eating or being given their favorite foods. Some parents are generous with or withhold food or food treats depending upon whether or not their children live up to their expectations. A dangerous connection has been created, and later in life when a young person feels unloved, he or she may turn to food and compulsive eating as a substitute for missing emotional support.

EATING OUT OF HABIT

Many people eat compulsively when they are engaged in some activity. You may nibble while you talk on the phone; you may eat while you do your homework. You may overeat when you go to the movies. It is behavior learned at home. You may have noticed that Mom gathered some snacks together when she made a long-distance call to her old college roommate, or that Dad raided the refrigerator before every football game on television. You may have noticed your parents' willingness to buy you treats whenever you went to the movies. And because it was rewarding, you continued the behavior yourself, mostly out of habit.

PRESSURE TO EAT

Some families use food as a way to manipulate each other.

> *Everyone in Amy's family was overweight, except for Amy. Amy was slender, and she didn't have to worry about what she ate. But her mother wasn't happy with her.*
>
> *"Oh, Amy," she said. "Why don't you eat something. You're too skinny."*
>
> *However, when Amy didn't gain weight, her mother started preparing her favorite desserts and leaving them around in plain sight. Amy found them hard to resist.*
>
> *Amy started to gain weight. Then, feeling unhappy with herself, she would stay home, which was just what her mother wanted.*

Amy's mother would say, "You are perfectly fine just the way you are."

Amy sometimes tried to break away from her family's grasp. She announced plans to attend a college out of state, but her mother soon became sick and asked her to pick a school closer to home in case she needed her.

When Amy started dating, her overweight sisters made fun of the guy Amy went out with and made fun of her for liking him. It soon became clear to Amy that her family seemed to like her only when she stayed home with them. It even occurred to her that they were encouraging her to overeat because they wanted her to feel unwanted, the way they did. That way, Amy would never leave home. Whereas Amy resisted, her sisters clearly had learned that "the family that eats together, stays together."

The causes of compulsive eating are not always so clearly defined. Some people may be emotional eaters who learned at an early age to turn to food. Behavior that has been learned and reinforced in the family is hard to change because people have to change their attitudes as well as their habits. But once you learn to recognize the pressure, you can begin to manage compulsive eating. In the next chapters, you will find specific ways to cure the problem or cope with it.

5 Causes and Solutions

It's difficult to say how many people are compulsive eaters because of innate biological factors. Nutritionists and doctors may be more likely to focus on biological causes than psychologists and psychiatrists. Compulsive eaters themselves may prefer to believe that there are physiological reasons for their behavior because these explanations don't involve their emotions. For many people, it's easier to take mineral supplements and prescription medications than it is to examine their own feelings.

Most compulsive eating, however, results from a combination of biological and psychological factors. Even if the cause of an eating disorder is psychological, poor nutrition can alter your thinking process. If you compulsively overeat, strong sugar fluctuations and mineral imbalances may lead to cravings.

Nutritional explanations for compulsive eating hold that people compulsively eat certain foods when their bodies are lacking key minerals. One example is if your diet is too high in calcium and too low in magnesium. We absorb calcium only when we take in more magnesium than calcium, so if the minerals are not in balance, we will be deficient in magnesium and the excess calcium becomes toxic. Imbalances in minerals can lead to food binges.

SUGAR CRAVINGS

If you are hypoglycemic, you may turn to foods with a high sugar content to ease the physical symptoms of low blood sugar. People with hypoglycemia have too little glucose in their bloodstream. Consequently, they get the "shakes" and may feel weak, dizzy, and sometimes depressed. Although eating the complex carbohydrates in ordinary food would eventually restore the correct sugar balance in a healthy way, it wouldn't correct their symptoms very quickly. Sugar provides the quick fix. When people eat sugar, the bloodstream gets a jolt of glucose. However, the pancreas has to secrete a larger than normal amount of insulin to process this sugar, and so the sugar is quickly used up.

Eating sugar, then, causes a rebound effect. Once you start eating it, you have to keep eating it because the symptoms of low blood sugar return so quickly. With hypoglycemia, your body has an abnormally high rate of metabolism, and you process sugar, as well as other foods, more quickly than you normally would. The effort to keep low blood sugar at bay by eating heavily sugared foods results in compulsive eating.

Hypoglycemia and sugar cravings can also result from insufficient amounts of chromium in your body. Chromium is a trace mineral that helps transport glucose into cell tissues. When chromium is in short supply, your body can become insulin-resistant. Insulin helps to process sugar in your body. Even though your pancreas secretes sufficient insulin, without chromium the cells won't use the insulin, and it will be excreted from the body. An imbalance in the body's processing of glucose, stemming from a shortage of chromium, will cause both hypoglycemic symptoms and sugar cravings.

Sugar cravings can also stem from a condition called candida, which is a yeast infection. Sugar feeds this yeast infection, so people with untreated yeast infections often crave huge amounts of sugar. Everyone harbors the organism *Candida albicans* in his or her body. If a person's body is in proper chemical balance, the candida doesn't become a problem. However, factors such as hormonal changes, diets rich in sugar, and long-term antibiotic use can upset the chemical balance and can cause the fungus candida to overrun the body. Compulsively eating sugary foods may trigger the candida overgrowth, as well as sustain it.

Solutions

Your nutritionist can give you advice on healthy eating habits and help you to decide if you need to take chromium or other dietary supplements. If sugar cravings are a result of an untreated yeast infection, the underlying infection must first be treated. Candida is treated with an antifungal medication available in drugstores without a prescription.

However, it's important to consult a doctor before taking any medication.

FOOD SENSITIVITIES AND ALLERGIES

People don't often think of sensitivities as causing us to eat more of a substance that can hurt us, but that's exactly what happens. Sensitivities to certain foods come in the form of allergies that cause hives, headaches, or bronchial spasms. Then people clearly know that they should avoid certain foods. However, food sensitivities don't always cause such clear-cut reactions.

If you have a food sensitivity, your body probably is not able to completely digest the food's proteins. When the proteins are not digested, the undigested molecules reach the tissues through the bloodstream. These undigested protein molecules look like foreign matter, and so your body produces antibodies to defend against them. The next time you eat this food, your immune system will attack the partially digested protein molecules as invaders. This is an allergic reaction, but instead of getting hives, you will start craving huge amounts of the very foods your body can't handle. Sugar and white flour are common problematic foods.

When you eat foods you are allergic to, you are more likely to catch viruses. Your immune system has been weakened in the process of fighting the alien protein molecules. People with food sensitivities often get headaches and feel tired without understanding that it's a result of a particular food that they have eaten. Then, ironically, they start compulsively eating more of the offending food.

Solutions

If a doctor or nutritionist suspects that you have either a sensitivity or an allergy, he will suggest that you eliminate all the possible allergic foods from your diet for a period of four weeks. This is called an elimination diet. If your symptoms disappear during the elimination diet, you probably have allergies or sensitivities to one of the foods you have eliminated.

To follow an elimination diet, you stop eating all the foods that contain the ingredients to which you're sensitive. That means that you have to read the list of ingredients every time you shop for a product. Finding a product that doesn't contain sugar or corn syrup (another form of sugar) can be harder than you realize—so you have to look carefully!

Foods to which you're sensitive can be reintroduced into your diet in small amounts once your body seems able to handle them. Foods to which you're actually allergic must be permanently eliminated from your diet. You may gradually discover that you feel much better when not eating these particular foods. Later, when you reintroduce these foods a little at a time, you may experience headaches, depression, and fatigue. At that point, you are fully aware of the consequences of eating foods to which you're sensitive. Other people may find that they can build up a tolerance to the offending foods so that indulging in them occasionally won't cause a chain reaction of discomfort and cravings.

Some women become compulsive eaters in the week preceding their periods. This probably reflects a hormonal imbalance that can be helped by eating foods that raise estrogen levels: milk products, eggs, and legumes. It's also important to maintain a sufficiently high magnesium level, not simply by taking vitamin and mineral supplements but by keeping the minerals in proper balance through your diet. A nutritionist can advise you on how to keep this balance, either through altering your diet or through vitamin and mineral supplements.

FOOD ADDICTIONS

Many people believe that we can become addicted to certain foods, especially to highly refined carbohydrates, chocolate, and caffeine. An addict is a person who continues to use a substance compulsively without caring about the negative consequences. He knows that what he is doing is harmful, but he continues to do it anyway. Food addiction is similar to alcohol and drug addiction in that it occurs in stages.

The first stage involves the person's preoccupation with the addiction. Whether a person has a food sensitivity or seeks food for comfort, she thinks about food most of the day. She may plan menus, cook meals for her family, or calculate how many calories she can safely handle that day. She may keep food in her room and eat when she's alone.

The second stage of the addiction occurs when the person has a hard time limiting the amount of food he consumes. The food addict may resort to deception to prevent others from suspecting his addiction. For example, if he buys a large quantity of food at the grocery store, he may tell people he's planning a party, although he may plan to eat the food himself. At this point, the food addict is experiencing the consequences of overeating. He is very likely overweight (unless he is purging). He is probably tired a lot and unhappy with himself.

This leads to the third and final stage of addiction: a loss of interest in anything other than food. The food addict may decline to go out and withdraw into himself. This isolation most likely reinforces his compulsive eating.

Some people think it's too drastic to consider a compulsive overeater to be an addict. They reason that the overeater is simply not controlling his appetite. The people who subscribe to the theory of addiction say that the compulsive overeater can't control his appetite. Like other addictions, food addiction has a physical basis and must be treated as such.

Managing Addictions

For people who appear to be addicted to sugar, treatment involves eliminating the foods the addict cannot handle, as well as involvement in a recovery support group such as Overeaters Anonymous. Groups like this help you to cope with abstinence from the food you're addicted to and to work through the emotional reasons for turning to food. These groups are usually free.

Many people believe that alcoholics have a different chemistry from their nonalcoholic peers. Alcoholics seem predisposed to lose control when they use certain substances that don't affect nonalcoholics in the same way. Some say that alco- holics are born that way, that they produce fewer endorphins (the body's natural pain-relieving chemicals), and the substances they abuse tend to restore their sense of well-being.

Food addicts appear to show the same type of behavior. They treat food the way an alcoholic treats alcohol. The more sweet or starchy foods they eat, the more they crave. Giving up sweets entirely is hard to do, which is why support groups are so helpful. All addictive behaviors have similar traits, so groups that recognize and try to deal with the overwhelming cravings that abstinent people still get are bound to be very helpful, no matter what the craving.

CHEMICAL IMBALANCES

Carbohydrate and sugar cravings can result from factors other than hypoglycemia. Low serotonin production can leave you craving carbohydrates. Serotonin is a chemical found in the brain that is needed for mood stability, control of impulsiveness, and control of appetite. Too little serotonin will cause depression, anger and irritability, sleep loss, and a craving for carbohydrates. That craving is the body's way of restoring its serotonin level, because the tryptophan in carbohydrates is one of the chem- ical building blocks of serotonin. Chromium supple- ments will help increase the amounts of tryptophan reaching the brain.

No tests exist to determine how much seroto- nin a person produces, but doctors can get a good idea from the symptoms produced and a person's response to a group of antidepressant medications called selective serotonin reuptake inhibitors (SSRIs). If you have a low level of serotonin, you are likely to have other symptoms besides carbohydrate cravings—usually depression and irritability. Again, the solution is to choose a diet rich in complex carbohydrates and to see a nutritionist for specific advice about vitamin and mineral supplements.

The main chemicals of the brain that have to do with mood, pleasure, pain, and eating disorders are serotonin, dopamine, norepinephrine, and endorphins. When endorphins are in low supply, the brain is "on edge." People may turn to mood-altering substances to soothe the brain artificially. That often means using alcohol and drugs, but some people choose food. Chocolate, sugar, and caffeine all contain substances that alter the levels of certain chemicals in the brain.

One of those chemicals, serotonin, is often called the calming chemical. When you have a sufficient amount of serotonin in your brain, you are not as likely to be depressed, you sleep better, and you have more control over compulsive eating as well as other compulsive behaviors.

Norepinephrine is another chemical closely linked to both mood and appetite. Sufficient amounts of norepinephrine signal the brain that you're hungry. Serotonin, in turn, tells the brain that you're full and can stop eating. Scientists have discovered that people who binge and purge have an unusually low level of serotonin. It's possible that they are not receiving messages from their brains that they are full, so they continue to overeat.

People with other types of compulsive behavior, like the symptoms common to obsessive-compulsive disorder (washing hands many times a day, checking to see if doors are locked, hoarding trash to excess), appear to respond to medications that raise the serotonin levels in the brain. With improved levels of this chemical, people seem better able to deal with their compulsions.

Because serotonin levels are important in helping us feel calm and in control, it's not surprising that people feel better when taking medications such as Prozac, Zoloft, and Paxil that increase serotonin levels. However, the carbohydrates in ordinary, healthy foods can also increase your serotonin level.

Antidepressant Medications

A person with a low serotonin level should respond to selective serotonin reuptake inhibitor (SSRI) medications, which are dispensed by a doctor. Other antidepressants increase levels of both serotonin and norepinephrine, with the result that people get hungry and gain weight.

Serotonin is produced in the brain's nerve cells and is released into the synapses (the spaces between the neurons). Then the chemical is absorbed back into the releasing neuron to be used again. The longer serotonin lingers in the synapse, the greater the effect on mood instability, depression, and appetite control. Thus, selective serotonin reuptake inhibitors slow the reabsorption of serotonin into the neuron, causing it to linger in the synapse longer. SSRIs include the drugs Prozac, Zoloft, Luvox, Paxil, and Effexor. These medications are very expensive. You could pay between $60 and $160 for a month's prescription.

People who take other antidepressant medications may find that they are hungry all the time or are simply putting on weight. The reason probably has to do with the chemicals in the brain that the specific antidepressants affect. Those that affect both norepinephrine and serotonin will cause more compulsive eating than the SSRIs that simply affect serotonin. That's because norepinephrine is the chemical that signals us that we're hungry. Serotonin signals us when we're full. Those antidepressants that target norepinephrine, such as the tricyclics, stimulate people's appetites. Asking your doctor to switch your antidepressant to a SSRI may help control your compulsive eating. Sometimes one antidepressant is preferred over another for reasons unrelated to appetite, so it's not a good idea to substitute your friend's antidepressant prescription for yours.

Sometimes tricyclic antidepressants have the opposite effect on appetite. As a rule, they stimulate appetite, but there is certainly plenty of anecdotal evidence that people taking antidepressants such as Imipramine can experience steady, healthy weight loss. In some cases, the medication alleviates depression. Emotional eaters who turn to food to deal with their sadness, start to feel less depressed, and as a result, stop overeating. The antidepressants actually help in regaining control of their appetite.

Restored levels of serotonin seem to be responsible for managing compulsive behavior in general. People who take Prozac or Luvox often gain control over obsessive/compulsive symptoms, such as excessive hand washing and checking to see that doors are locked. Many doctors suspect a link between obsessive/compulsive behavior and compulsive eating.

DIETING AND OVEREATING

You might think that dieting is the solution rather than the cause of compulsive eating, but in reality dieting is a major trigger for the behaviors associated with compulsive eating. Bingeing during diets isn't necessarily a result of a lack of discipline or self-control, either. There are biological reasons why people who are on restrictive diets and are consuming less that the recommended daily allowance of calories are more likely to go on eating binges. Let's take a look at the example of Alan.

Alan waged a constant battle with his weight. He ate a lot of sugar, so he started drinking diet colas and skipping desserts, but it didn't seem to help control his weight. He didn't realize that caffeinated drinks can set off sugar cravings just as easily as sugar-sweetened drinks can. Finally, he decided that he couldn't manage his weight by dieting unless he was either very strict or simply went on a fast.

He tried a rigid diet first. The first week went pretty well. As long as he didn't eat anything not on the diet, he didn't crave the forbidden foods. Of course, he made excuses not to eat lunch with his friends because he couldn't eat his salads without wanting their french fries. By the second week, he was feeling deprived and finally gave in to the urge to eat "just one little french fry." He ultimately ate much more than a regular meal since he was so starved.

"Diets don't work for me," he thought. "When I sit around other people, I want what they're eating. If I eat just one thing, I start craving a whole pile of food. Maybe I should fast."

Fasting allowed Alan to feel good about skipping meals. After all, he reasoned, he was purifying his system. On the days he didn't fast, he reasoned that he could eat anything he wanted. He tried fasting one day a week, but he quickly began to dread Tuesdays, the day he had chosen to fast. The more he tried not to think about food, the more he thought about it.

The fast ended one night when he stayed up late studying. He had gone the whole day depriving himself and was undernourished. By 10:00 PM he was raiding the refrigerator, consoling himself that he'd fasted all day. It was always following a fast that Alan overate the most.

There's a biological reason for overeating after a fast. Dieting sets us up for low blood sugar and extreme hunger. Feeling weak and dizzy makes us want to do whatever it takes to remedy the situation. We need a quick fix, and heavily sugared foods are the best choice for raising blood-sugar levels quickly. Unfortunately, that activates the rebound effect, and we have to spend the next hour or two pumping ourselves full of sugar.

Extreme hunger, the result of fasting, leads us to binge eating. We are simply so hungry that we don't pay any attention to how much we are taking in. Hurried eating leads to eating more than our bodies need.

Do Diets Work?

*P*atty *thought that she needed to lose weight because her compulsive eating had resulted in her being sixty pounds overweight. She didn't have the money to join a weight-loss program, and her parents couldn't afford to buy her the special food. So she decided to create her own diet, using liquid supplements and fasting.*

Friends told her to fast first because it would rid her body of toxins and make it easier to stay on a diet. "After all, anything will taste great when all you've had is apple juice," one friend said. So Patty spent the first day fasting. When she felt an overwhelming desire to eat something, she drank apple juice. She soon was sick of apple juice, and water didn't seem to taste as good after she had forced herself to drink eight tall glasses a day.

However, Patty kept seeing pictures of herself as a slim model, and so she stuck to the fast. The next day she drank three chocolate malt diet drinks, and although they tasted better, she actually missed chewing food. By dinnertime, when she was supposed to eat a regular meal, she was so hungry for something to chew that she feared going overboard. So she substituted another liquid diet drink for her regular dinner.

The next day she saw that she had lost three pounds, and she was so elated that she decided to skip her third diet drink that day. For dinner that night, she ate potatoes and vegetables and a small piece of chicken. The next day, those three pounds had returned.

"I guess I have to be more strict with my regular meals," she told herself. That night she ate a couple of pieces of lettuce and some sugar-free Jell-O. Her parents had left early for a meeting and had no idea how poorly she was eating.

Patty found herself thinking more and more about food, and the more she thought about the things she was missing, the more she felt she had to punish herself. She ate less and less at each regular meal. On the day she was supposed to give a speech in history class, she stood up and fainted. Because her heartbeat was erratic, school nurses called an ambulance to take her to the hospital.

A CRITICAL LOOK AT DIETING

Dieting is a big industry. The diet business is hard to ignore—it advertises on billboards, on television, and in the newspapers. Hundreds of products are on the market claiming to help people lose weight:

over-the-counter diuretics (drugs that make your body excrete water); liquid meals; and appetite suppressants that speed up your body's metabolism. Some companies create diet groups that model themselves after support groups. In these groups, the participants rally each other as they try to lose weight, and usually weigh in at certain intervals to check their progress.

Some of these approaches to dieting are healthier than others. Belonging to a group of people who support each other is healthier than simply popping diet pills. But all diet product manufacturers have two things in common. First, they are businesses, and like any other business, they provide services in order to make a profit from customers (that's you). Secondly, they encourage you to measure your success according to how much weight you lose.

There are serious problems with this dieting model. First, since their business depends on the success of their products (and your subsequent weight loss), diet companies tend to emphasize strict regimens and short-term solutions. People are impatient. If you don't see a rapid change in your weight, you will assume that the product doesn't work and stop spending your money on it. Short-term solutions may produce some immediate loss of weight, but the weight is regained as soon as you go off that particular diet.

Second, the above pattern of dieting, of short-term weight loss followed by a weight increase, exasperation, and changing to a new diet, only reinforces your thoughts about food. If you go off a diet, you may feel that you have failed. To make up for your bad feelings, you may try to restrict yourself in other ways or engage in some other unhealthy behavior. Binge eating often results from failed diets. As a rule, strict dieting only reinforces compulsive eating.

Diets aren't useful for compulsive eaters because losing weight isn't the issue. As you know from reading earlier chapters, compulsive eating is caused by a variety of factors and doesn't always result in weight gain. When you focus on losing a certain amount of weight, you lose sight of the bigger picture—the purpose that food has been serving for you. Furthermore, people who are intent on losing weight, particularly within a certain time frame, may be tempted to try medically unsafe diets, with disastrous results.

So we have to look at diets with a great deal of skepticism. There are individuals who diet successfully, lose weight, maintain their new weight, and are quite happy with the results of their diet. For the most part, however, these are people who, after dieting, are able to adjust their attitudes toward food in some way and eat in healthier ways. They may have been true victims of laziness and gluttony, so to speak, and all they needed to do was to lose a few pounds to get back on track. Such people probably do not suffer from strong connections between emotions and food. They were never compulsive eaters to begin with. And we all know that diet success stories like these are very rare.

Most people who go on crash diets or fad diets end up severely disappointed. Weight loss is followed by weight gain as soon as the diet stops, because the underlying cause has not been dealt with, and all that is accomplished is to increase a person's sense of failure and worthlessness. There is probably not a single reader of this book who cannot tell the story of some friend who has tried one of the new wonder diets and failed to lose weight for more than a short time. The simple truth is, in spite of new claims made every year, that unless the underlying reasons for compulsive eating are dealt with, in most cases diets do not work.

Diets are not the answer to compulsive eating problems, but there are solutions. First, you have to realize that there are a variety of reasons for over-eating or bingeing and purging. Make an appointment with a doctor and a nutritionist experienced in eating disorders. They can run tests to see if hormones or chemical imbalances are contributing to your eating problem. Successfully handling your compulsive eating means responding to the cause.

7 Physiological Consequences of Compulsive Eating

Sugar abuse is one consequence of eating compulsively. When people eat nutritious food, the nutrients are changed into glucose, which the body uses for fuel. The pancreas releases insulin to help process the glucose in the bloodstream and to get it into the cells and muscles. When you eat foods high in sugar, you get a quick jolt of sugar that goes right into the bloodstream. All that sugar triggers the pancreas to produce a larger than normal amount of insulin. The insulin quickly takes care of the sugar, and the blood glucose level drops quickly. This is called the crave/crash syndrome. People binge on sugar, and then feel awful once the insulin has processed the sugar out of the bloodstream. Then they want more sugar.

Sugar abuse can lead to two dangerous conditions: hypoglycemia and diabetes. Hypoglycemia occurs when the sugar is processed so quickly (because of abnormal amounts of insulin) that it leads to an abrupt drop in the blood glucose level.

People who eat a lot of sugar and then vomit often develop hypoglycemia. That's because their bodies produce a greater amount of insulin to take care of the large amount of sugar they consume. When they vomit up the food (and sugar), that excessive amount of insulin remains in the body. Now it doesn't have any sugar to process. People with hypoglycemia can feel shaky, dizzy, cold, and clammy. They may experience anxiety or rapid mood changes. The low blood glucose level makes them want more sugar, but the high amounts of sugar trigger higher amounts of insulin to deal with them, and the cycle is continued.

Diabetes is a life-threatening medical condition. Sometimes it is hereditary, but it can also result from sugar abuse. After being routinely called upon to secrete excess insulin in response to sugar, the pancreas simply wears out. When it stops producing insulin, the body is unable to process the sugar. That's why diabetics need either oral medication to correct their imbalance or insulin shots to supply what their bodies can't produce.

Diabetes is a permanent condition as well. If not properly treated, a diabetic faces many medical complications. If he gets too much insulin, he can go into insulin shock and die. Before he gets to that point, though, he may look and act oddly. He may become combative and not recognize his loved ones. If he has too much sugar (and isn't given insulin), he can fall into a coma and die.

Sugar abuse leads to other problems. You probably already know that too much sugar leads to tooth decay, even if you brush your teeth three times a day. But most people don't know that too much sugar can lead to a calcium deficiency. The body needs calcium for strong bones, but sugar imbalances can cause the body to give up its calcium, which is deposited in the form of kidney stones.

THE PHYSICAL EFFECTS OF BINGEING AND PURGING

Although in general compulsive eaters do not purge after a binge, some compulsive eaters occasionally do throw up either deliberately or from being overfull. Many bulimics may have started out as compulsive eaters, which indicates that compulsive eaters are at risk for developing bulimic behavior as a way of dealing with their binges. In any case, the risks and long-term effects of bingeing and purging are something compulsive eaters should be aware of.

The cycle of bingeing and purging has many medical consequences. People who purge by vomiting may find themselves vomiting after every meal, whether they want to or not. After months of vomiting several times a day, the body reflexively vomits after anything goes down the throat. This acquired response to food intake can lead to malnutrition.

Excessive vomiting also causes other problems. Bringing up your stomach contents is a forceful job, and it can damage the stomach. Stomach contents are very acidic (acid in the stomach helps digest food), and you run the risk of damaging the esophagus. People who throw up a lot may get a "chipmunk" look, because their cheeks swell. Stomach acid also erodes the enamel on their teeth. In severe cases, the throat bleeds.

Whether people purge by vomiting or using laxatives, the biggest risk is dehydration. When it's dehydrated, the body has lost fluids, and important minerals have been washed out along with the fluids. The skin dries out and loses its elasticity. Hair loses its shine. The contents of the digestive tract dry out as well, which causes constipation. Dehydration also leads to a mineral imbalance in the body, which causes bloating, abdominal pain, and gas. Whereas bloating and abdominal pain will make you feel uncomfortable, continued dehydration could lead to kidney failure and cardiac arrest.

Long-term laxative use has an effect on the body opposite to that caused by excessive vomiting. Excessive vomiting causes a reflexive reaction; a person vomits more easily after practice. Using a lot of laxatives causes the colon to lose its ability to move on its own; it becomes dependent upon the laxatives. Unfortunately, the quantity of laxatives required increases over time, which leads to dehydration and potassium loss.

COMPULSIVE EATING WITHOUT PURGING

Compulsive overeating can cause several serious medical problems. One of the most common results of overeating is obesity, which puts a tremendous strain on the heart and complicates all other medical conditions. If a person eats a lot of high-fat foods, she is likely to end up with high blood pressure, which is a major cause of strokes. If a person eats sugary foods, as mentioned before, she also risks developing hypoglycemia or diabetes.

Overweight people are also more prone to injury because they weigh more than their bodies can adequately support. Being overweight contributes to back problems and can cause respiratory problems. Whenever overweight people have surgery, they are at greater risk. They are also candidates for sleep apnea, a life-threatening condition in which excess skin in the throat interferes with breathing after a person falls asleep at night. When someone with this condition lies on his back, either his tongue or the excess skin falls into the back of his throat, obstructing the airway, and he stops breathing. After several seconds, the oxygen level in his blood drops and the person gulps in a fresh supply of air, waking himself in the process. This scenario replays itself as often as three hundred times a night, preventing the person from getting a full night's sleep.

Obesity is also connected to fertility problems. If an extremely overweight woman gets pregnant, the pregnancy is considered high risk. She will have to be monitored closely to make sure that both she and the baby do well.

Whether or not you are overweight, if you are a compulsive eater, you probably are very uncomfortable around food in public. You may try to avoid occasions and places where food will be present. Parties, banquets, dinners, and proms are all difficult occasions for compulsive eaters because they involve food. When you do go out, you may decline to eat anything. Compulsively controlling your behavior around food can lead to binge eating later on.

Compulsive eating is also influenced by social values. American society places a premium on attractiveness, and part of being attractive is being thin—even thinner than is healthy or normal. Therefore, people who are overweight are not considered attractive or appealing. Because society generally deems them undesirable, they are often ostracized.

This treatment has lasting consequences for someone's self-image and self-esteem. It also plays a part in developing or maintaining an eating disorder.

Getting Professional Help

If you think you may be a compulsive eater, it is important that you look for help. You may feel too ashamed to admit your problem to someone else, or you may want to keep your overeating a secret, hoping that it will go away on its own. Please remember, though, that shame and secrecy are two indicators of compulsive eating and that no problem ever disappears if you don't face it honestly. Asking for help is not a sign of weakness. It is a way of showing that you love yourself and are ready to trust others to help you become the best person you can be.

TREATMENT OPTIONS

There are many different programs and techniques designed to treat compulsive eating. Each one has a different approach. It is important to find the program that's right for you. Some people overcome overeating by reading self-help books. There are many books available in your local library or bookstore. You will find helpful resources at the end of this book as well. Other people, though, may feel that their compulsive eating is really out of control. In that case, a person should consider seeing a therapist and a registered dietitian for help.

Most dietitians will help you to relearn your internal hunger signals. They will work with you in individual counseling sessions. This process takes time, but many people have been treated successfully. The therapist will help you uncover some of the reasons behind your compulsive eating. Eating disorders are complex problems. They are caused by a combination of many factors, including psychological issues, biological changes, family influences, and messages from society.

The first thing you should do is talk to someone you trust. This person might be a friend, a parent, a sibling, or a teacher. If there is something going on in your life that is bothering you or causing you pain, tell that person about it. He or she will listen without judging you and will help you as much as possible.

You may find it easier to accept help from someone you don't know personally. Your school guidance office is a good place to start. Guidance counselors are caring people who understand the difficulties faced by teens. Food-related problems have become common among teenagers, and many guidance counselors are now quite knowledgeable about compulsive eating. If not, your guidance counselor will be able to direct you to a specialist. The counselor may also suggest a support group where you can meet other teens who share your problems and concerns. Support groups are important because they help people to understand that they are not alone in facing their problems.

Recovering from an eating disorder is like fighting an addiction to drugs or alcohol. It is a long, slow, and difficult process, and it may never be 100 percent complete. A recovering alcoholic will always have to be careful. Even if she hasn't had a drink in years, she may always have a strong urge to drink. People with eating disorders also have ongoing struggles and may relapse many times. But with treatment, many people do recover and go on to lead happy, fulfilling lives. If you are suffering from compulsive eating, please consider getting help.

THERAPY

If you are hesitant to go to a professional, please remember that many people eat compulsively because of unresolved emotional conflicts. Self-help books can pinpoint the problems for you, but sometimes you need to sit down and talk those problems out. It takes a great deal of courage to seek help. Going to a therapist or counselor does not mean you are crazy, nor does it mean that you are too weak to handle your problems yourself. These attitudes are false. Therapy helps you to live a good life under very trying circumstances.

People who eat compulsively benefit from therapy because they may also demonstrate other forms of compulsive behavior. Compulsive eaters may also be compulsive shoppers, drinkers, or exercisers. Obsessive/compulsive traits respond well to a therapy regimen of medication (usually SSRIs) and behavior modification. The medication helps to curb the compulsive behavior. Behavioral therapy helps the individual to make positive changes in the way she has dealt with compulsions in the past. Sometimes group treatment for compulsive behavior is the most helpful of all because other individuals with similar compulsions can share their insights and strategies.

Bingeing and purging can also stem from sexual abuse and early trauma. Both require therapy to help the individual recover and move on with her life. When people have been abused, they sometimes turn to compulsive eating to comfort themselves. Food also serves as the focus of their days, temporarily enabling them to avoid thinking about the source of their pain.

Treatment for chronic trauma, such as sexual abuse, first involves establishing a safe emotional environment, obtaining support from at least one person you have confidence in, learning when to trust and when not to trust others, and taking care of yourself. Once this basic need for emotional security is met, it is possible to explore past trauma while monitoring and stabilizing patterns of compulsive eating. The victim needs to learn that he was not to blame for the abuse and that he must move on with his life.

Types of Therapists

When you realize that your compulsive eating is caused by emotional conflicts, you may consider professional counseling. But who is the best person to see?

An eating disorder program or a therapist who specializes in eating disorders is best, because the professionals in this field have extensive training and experience in treating these conditions. You can check with hospitals in your area to learn if they have an eating disorder program or if they can recommend therapists who specialize in treating eating disorders. Sometimes these are listed in the Yellow Pages.

Your second choice is to find a qualified professional who takes clients with compulsive eating disorders. But which type of professional is best? Different professionals are good for different reasons. A psychiatrist is a doctor with a medical degree who is licensed to prescribe medication. If your compulsive eating stems from a chemical imbalance or physical disorder, he or she is the only one who can order medicine for your condition. A psychiatrist is the most expensive person to consult. Most people can't afford weekly visits to a psychiatrist unless their health insurance covers this type of care.

Primary care doctors may sometimes prescribe medication for compulsive overeating, but if they suspect another type of disorder, such as an endocrine disorder, they will usually refer the individual to another doctor, such as an endocrinologist, for a more elaborate examination.

Psychologists are professionals who have a doctoral degree in clinical psychology or in counseling psychology. Although some psychologists have only a master's degree in psychology, in the future most will be required to have a doctorate. As a general rule, the more credentials the therapist has, the more costly the appointment. Psychologists usually focus on nonmedical ways of dealing with problems. A psychologist's goal is to help you uncover your own reasons for doing things and to help you come up with ways that you can change unhealthy patterns of behavior.

Clinical social workers are therapists with either a doctorate in social work or a master of social work (MSW) degree. Some people, called licensed professional counselors, do the same work as clinical social workers but have graduate degrees in related mental health fields. A clinical social worker's approach will also be nonmedical and will be more dedicated to developing ways for you to help yourself.

Clinical psychiatric nurses are therapists with a master's degree in nursing. They can be particularly helpful in the treatment of eating disorders because, as nurses, they are well aware of the physical consequences of compulsive eating and purging.

THINGS TO CONSIDER WHEN CHOOSING A THERAPIST

Three factors come into play when considering which type of professional therapist you should choose.

⊙ Choose a professional who is licensed. Anyone in private practice or anyone who accepts third-party reimbursement (payment from insurance companies) will be licensed as a rule. Licensure means that the person has passed the required courses of instruction, has been supervised for the required number of hours, and has passed a state or national exam.

⊙ Choose a therapist whose style fits your personality. That doesn't mean you have to like everything your therapist does. Looking at problems is hard work, and most people resist it at some point. A therapist's job is to explore your situation and keep you focused on the task at hand. You won't always like that, and it's not meant to be fun. However, some therapists fit better with certain clients than others. It's more a matter of personality than how qualified they are. It is important that you feel safe and comfortable with your therapist. You should be able to talk freely with this person without feeling embarrassed, threatened, or ignored.

⊙ A good therapist will respect boundaries. Therapy is a working relationship. If your therapist suggests anything else, switch therapists or consult another therapist about the appropriateness of the treatment.

Other counselors exist to help people with their problems, but they are better suited to different problems. For example, school counselors are a logical choice for school-related difficulties. Certified alcohol and drug counselors are good choices for people who have substance-abuse problems in addition to problems with compulsive eating. You may find people in your church, temple, or mosque who could be helpful to you as well.

SPECIALIZED EATING DISORDER PROGRAMS

As a rule, people with eating disorders (bingeing and purging or compulsive eating) respond best to trained professionals who have experience treating eating disorders. It's true that some people need their depression treated before they can make progress on their compulsive eating, but it's much more difficult to get rid of one problem without addressing the other. Compulsive eating still needs to be addressed and managed even if the under-lying depression must be taken care of first. A therapist who is familiar with eating disorders or compulsive behavior may be more useful than the therapist who treats only depression.

Bulimics, or people who binge and purge, are seriously hurting their bodies. Hospitalization is usually necessary to repair physical damage and to get the compulsive eating under control.

A structured eating disorder program includes individual therapy, group therapy, and family therapy. Some doctors will prescribe medication if they think that the patient has a chemical imbalance that is partly responsible for the bingeing behavior. The program's staff will also monitor the patient's eating and educate him about the damage he's doing to his body.

Group therapy appears to be the most effec-tive type of therapy for people with serious eating disorders because patients can learn just as much from their peers as they can from the therapist. The issues for patients who binge and purge are rarely about food. Focusing on food (how much the individual eats, how much she vomits, how many laxatives she uses or refrains from using) keeps the spotlight off the other issues in a person's life.

OVEREATERS ANONYMOUS

Many support groups are formulated on twelve-step programs and, like Alcoholics Anonymous and Al-Anon, are highly successful in helping people manage their compulsive behavior. Some people can find help for their compulsions through therapy, but they still have trouble fully controlling themselves. They may know why they focus on food, but they are ineffective in changing their habits.

> *Aretha was both severely depressed and a compulsive eater. She got into therapy and worked hard to resolve her feelings of emptiness and rage, stemming from early physical and sexual abuse at the hands of her stepfather and an elderly baby-sitter. Although Aretha made a lot of progress in therapy, she still couldn't seem to stop overeating. In fact, she often compulsively stole food from the local grocery store.*
>
> *She rationalized what she did: "The lines were too long at the checkout counter, so I just walked out with the stuff." Or she would say, "I didn't have enough money for the food right then, and I figured I could pay it back later*

when I got my check."

Exploring Aretha's compulsive stealing as well as her compulsive eating had little effect on her behavior. What eventually helped her was joining Overeaters Anonymous, where she found many people like herself. "Other people steal food, too," she marveled. "It's part of our addictive cycle."

Aretha found a sponsor and called her when she found herself headed out the door to the grocery store. "I just couldn't control the behavior by myself," she said. "Therapy gave me the tools to examine my past and what I was doing, but Overeaters Anonymous gave me the support to actually resist the behavior."

People who determine that their compulsive eating is a form of addictive behavior will benefit from groups like Overeaters Anonymous (OA). These support groups are run by people with similar addictions. They offer emotional support, acceptance and understanding, and a strategy for coping with an addiction. They recognize that certain occasions pose more of a problem than others for the food addict, and they offer advice on how to get through these occasions.

Sometimes groups like OA are all the support a person needs to change her behavior. At other times OA is a supplement to regular therapy. Both OA and therapy are helpful in managing aspects of compulsive eating. There is no minimum age for joining OA. Anyone who feels that he or she has trouble controlling his or her behavior around food can join.

If you can't find an OA group in your area

(they're usually listed in the phone book), you can write to the address listed in the Where to Go for Help section at the end of this book for the name and number of the closest group.

THE DIFFERENCE BETWEEN OA AND DIET GROUPS

Some people join diet groups to gain control over their compulsive eating. If dieting were the answer, these support groups would be more helpful. However, the problem is not that you weigh too much. People who binge and purge don't necessarily need to lose weight; they are probably of average size. When you join a weight-loss group, the focus is on losing weight, and you are supported in your efforts to control your intake and shed unwanted pounds.

Overeaters Anonymous is a better alternative, for it focuses on helping you to recover physically and emotionally from compulsive overeating. The focus is on what is causing your eating patterns instead of on your weight.

When a Friend Is a Compulsive Eater

If you think a friend or family member is a compulsive eater, talk to him or her about it. Speak in a way that is loving and supportive, and let the person know that you are there to help. Share some of the information you have learned in this book about compulsive eating. If you want to know more, try contacting some of the organizations listed in the back of this book.

Because facing such a difficult problem can be extremely painful, your friend or loved one may not be willing to accept your help when it is first offered. Don't be hurt if the person becomes angry or resentful, and don't try to force that person to accept your help immediately. Unfortunately, you cannot force a person to get help if he or she does not want it or is not ready for it. If that happens, offer to continue to listen and care, and perhaps one day that person will be ready to talk openly about his or her feelings and take that first step toward recovery. Here are things you can do to support a friend who is dealing with an eating disorder.

- Never nag your friend about her weight or her compulsive eating. Nagging doesn't get anyone to change his or her behavior, but it does produce resentment. Resentment often leads to acting out the very behavior you are trying to change. If your friend brings up the subject of her eating habits, all you really need to do is listen.

- Don't socialize with food around all the time. Choose other activities for your friend that don't involve eating. You will be helping to break your friend's compulsive patterns. Just try not to make a big deal out of it.

- Remain nonjudgmental, even if your friend decides that he doesn't want to take control of his compulsive eating. If you judge him, you will find him lacking, and he will sense this. Sensing your disapproval, he may feel bad about himself and find it even harder to get control of his behavior. Or he may be angry that he feels he has to live up to your expectations.

- Never offer your friend advice unless he asks for it. If he's really asking for your advice, he will say, "What do you think?" Even then, be careful what you say. If you jump in too quickly with a solution, you may find that he has changed his mind in the meantime and doesn't want advice anymore. If he does ask you for advice, describe how you see the problem without being judgmental. Be careful not to play therapist. Simply tell him what you see. You can say, "I think you lose control around food and eat things that aren't always healthy."

⊙ If your friend decides that she wants to join a support group but is afraid to go alone the first time, offer to go with her. Chances are that she will meet other people like herself and won't need you to keep going with her. But you will be helping her to get to that first meeting. Don't suggest attending the meeting if she hasn't decided that it is right for her.

⊙ Don't make a big deal out of your own weight, especially if it's more normal than your friend's. Don't talk endlessly about dieting.

WHEN IT'S IMPORTANT TO ACT

Although, as we've said before, most compulsive eaters don't purge by throwing up or using laxatives, there is a strong chance that the disordered behaviors of compulsive eating could turn into bulimia.

Sheila knew that her friend Roxanne was throwing up after eating in order to lose weight for the prom. She had heard Roxanne in the bathroom throwing up after eating some chips one night when she stayed over at Sheila's house. Sheila didn't know what to say or do. Should she tell Roxanne's mother or should she leave well enough alone? She decided to wait and see if this behavior continued.

A week later, the girls went out to eat pizza. When Roxanne excused herself after eating to go to the bathroom, Sheila sneaked into the bathroom after her. She heard Roxanne throwing up again. When Roxanne came out of the stall to wash her face, Sheila was standing there at the sink.

"Roxanne, you're bulimic, aren't you? How long have you been doing this?"

Startled, Roxanne put her hands over her face. "Don't tell anyone. It was only this one time."

"No, it isn't," Sheila said. "I heard you throwing up over at my house the other night."

"I only do it once in a while," Roxanne pleaded. "I'm not bulimic."

"You need to get some help," Sheila said, but she really didn't know what kind of help Roxanne needed.

"I'm just doing this to help lose some weight. I'm really okay."

Sheila walked out as a couple of other people came into the bathroom. She really thought that she should do something, but she didn't want to betray her friend.

She avoided Roxanne for the next couple of weeks, but when Roxanne fainted during gym class, Sheila knew that she had to do more than just watch her friend get more and more sick.

Sheila went to her gym teacher and said, "I think you should know that Roxanne is throwing up after she eats. She has been doing this for several weeks but she won't get help."

Sheila looked at the floor. "She told me not to tell."

"Bulimia is a life-threatening condition," the teacher said.

"But I wasn't sure she had that," Sheila said.

The gym teacher saw how concerned Sheila was. "It's hard to know when a friend should tell on a friend," she said. "In some cases, that's the best thing a friend can do."

It can be very difficult to tell if a friend is bulimic or a compulsive eater. What follows is a list of some telltale physical signs of bulimia:

- ⊙ Chipmunk cheeks. Puffy cheeks are an indication that a person is vomiting regularly.

- ⊙ Scrapes on the knuckles of the hands. When forcing themselves to throw up, bulimics often scrape their knuckles on their teeth.

- ⊙ Bloodshot eyes or burst blood vessels in the eyes. This is another common sign of repeated vomiting.

⊙ Frequent trips to the bathroom
directly after eating.

⊙ Bad breath.

In many instances, these physical clues may be the only outward differences between compulsive eaters and bulimics. Both types of disordered eating are unhealthy, and both usually indicate very deep emotional problems and lack of self-esteem.

Under no circumstances should you play therapist with your friend. Even professional therapists don't counsel their friends. That's because you are so involved with the person that you can't be objective about her condition. You also don't have the experience or training that a professional does. You can listen to your friend's problems, and you can empathize with her, but you can't make her well.

If your friend is a compulsive eater whose health is compromised by her overeating, you have to get through to her that it's her health that concerns you, not her appearance. You want to convey concern, not judgment. Ultimately, each person has to make up his or her own mind about getting control over compulsive eating. If you find yourself continually interfering, your friend is not ready to make changes. It's only when people are interested in changing that they will pick up a book like this one. That's a start. Your job is to stand on the sidelines and support your friend's efforts. If she slips up, don't lecture. Keep offering support. Let her know that you are there if she needs you.

10 Dealing with Compulsive Eating

After reading the previous chapters, you are probably beginning to get a sense of how compulsive eating works—what the behaviors are, what underlying emotional reasons there may be for the behaviors, what biological factors aggravate those behaviors, and what the physical consequences of these behaviors are. If you are a compulsive eater, you may be wondering what the next step is. How do you help yourself?

Once you know that your compulsive eating doesn't stem from a physical cause, or once you have taken steps to correct the physical aspect of the problem, you are ready to look at your emotional relationship to food. The emotional reasons for compulsive eating may not be easy to identify, so this is when you need to do some good detective work.

IDENTIFYING UNHEALTHY PATTERNS OF BEHAVIOR

A food diary is a good way to identify the kinds of circumstances in which you overeat or eat unhealthy things. There are two ways to keep a food diary. You can make a diary out of an ordinary notebook by writing down three headings: What I Ate, How Much I Ate, and What Feeling or Situation Triggered the Eating. You must be diligent about writing down everything you eat. It's usually the stuff that you don't think is significant that counts. If it's too scary to record everything you eat in a day, make an effort to record as much as possible.

The other way to keep track of the food you eat, and the situations that prompt you to overeat, is simply to draw circles in your notebook to represent how much you ate on a certain day. Bigger circles represent bigger meals, including your regular mealtimes. People who snack a lot may have several smaller circles spread out over the page. In the circles, write down the times that you ate.

After a week or two of keeping a food diary (and it may not take that long to see your patterns), you will be able to make connections between what and when you eat and how you're feeling. Once you have made that connection, you can decide how to handle the problem. Remember, the idea of keeping a food diary is not to make you feel worse by showing how much you eat. It is simply a tool that can show you how you are using food in an unhealthy way.

RECOGNIZING TRIGGERS

A food diary can show three things: how certain circumstances will trigger eating when you are not hungry, how certain feelings can trigger eating, and how ingrained habits can make you want to eat. Once you recognize the triggers, you can learn ways to avoid them. Avoiding them altogether is easier than trying to ignore the triggers once they're activated. For example, Julie realized that she couldn't walk past the bakery on her way home without wanting to go inside and buy a pastry. The problem was that she couldn't buy just one pastry; she would buy a dozen. She would feel guilty after she had eaten a couple of the pastries, but she couldn't bring herself to throw the rest away because she had spent so much money on them. But if Julie doesn't walk past the bakery in the first place, she has no desire to buy any pastries. In her case, she curbed much of her afternoon snacking simply by taking another route home.

Avoiding triggers is called breaking behavioral chains. You may have gotten into the habit of eating around certain people or in certain situations. It has nothing to do with being hungry. You get used to eating pizza with friends on Friday night; you get used to eating your way through the store when you go grocery shopping; and you binge when you find open bags of cookies or candy bars in the cupboard. It may be easier to stave off a binge if you don't put yourself in the situation that triggers compulsive behavior.

If you always eat with certain friends, try a different activity. If your friends are not supportive of your change in eating habits, avoid these people, because they will most likely hurt your efforts. If you can't walk past stores without buying binge foods, avoid being near the stores. Ask someone else in your family to do the grocery shopping.

If you are the type of person who can manage her cravings just fine as long as trigger situations don't present themselves, you must make the effort to avoid all associations with certain foods, people, and situations.

FOOD AND YOUR FEELINGS

If you are a compulsive eater, chances are that you are much kinder to and more supportive of other people than you are to yourself. Compulsive eaters suffer from low self-esteem; they don't always believe in their own value as human beings. Be aware of when you are being unkind to yourself and work on changing your attitude. Here are four ways to avoid negative thinking:

⊙ DON'T criticize yourself! It's difficult to make your life better tomorrow if you hate who you are today. The next time you find yourself saying or thinking something unkind about yourself or your body, stop and think whether you would ever say such a mean thing to a family member or a friend. Chances are you wouldn't. You probably don't like to hurt other people's feelings, so why hurt your own? Try to be more aware of frustrating, self-critical thoughts, and take a moment to apologize to yourself when you hurt yourself. Also try to admire yourself for the good qualities you have that don't revolve around appearance, such as intelligence, generosity, thoughtfulness, kindness, and a sense of humor.

⊙ DON'T compare yourself to others! To the compulsive eater, other people always seem thinner, happier, and more successful. Thin people seem to live easy lives, free of the pain and shame that the compulsive eater must cope with every day. However, remember that appearances can be deceiving. All people experience struggles and suffer disappointments, but you can't always see this in the people you admire or envy.

⊙ DON'T worry about what other people think! Compulsive eaters spend too much time and energy thinking about other people's opinions, real or imagined. They assume the worst, believing that others will probably reject them or make fun of them because they're fat. This negative view often prevents compulsive eaters from meeting new friends and participating in interesting activities that they want to try. Some people may treat you badly because of your weight, but others won't. Focus on the people you meet who don't seem concerned about your weight. There will always be unhappy people in the world who feel the need to reject or abuse anyone who is different, but most people are more open-minded and caring. Besides, it's impossible to know what everyone else thinks and feels about us. Even if we did know, we couldn't necessarily control or change it. All that time worrying about who likes you and who doesn't like you is better spent learning to love and care for yourself and finding friends who like you for who you are.

⊙ DON'T live in the future! Nearly every compulsive eater thinks, "If only I were thin!" They dream of some magical day in the future when they will wake up and find themselves thin and happy. They believe that all of their problems would disappear if they could just lose weight and keep it off. Sadly, this is a false hope. If you are a compulsive eater, you must learn to live in the present instead of living for the future, and that means finding a way to love, respect, and accept the most important person in your life: the person you are today! That also means understanding that thinness does not equal happiness.

RESPECT YOUR OWN FEELINGS

The majority of emotional eaters binge to cover up their feelings. Some people binge when they're angry, some when they're depressed, and others when they're anxious. Compulsive eaters may also eat as a way of ignoring or devaluing their own feelings. They may eat, knowing they shouldn't, as a way of insulting themselves or putting themselves down for feeling a certain way.

Loneliness

"Everybody at school seems to have a boy-friend or girlfriend, but nobody will ever love me because I'm fat and ugly."

"You can't trust people anyway. They are never there for you when you need them. Food is the one thing I can count on in my life."

Many compulsive eaters have not experienced enough love in their lives, so they begin to think of food as love. They may grow up in families where everybody is expected to be an overachiever, and they feel pressured to be perfect. Or their parents or brothers and sisters may be overly critical, always pointing out what is wrong with them and never what is right. In still other instances, family members are not allowed to recognize or express their emotions, particularly feelings of warmth and affection. When people do not have a chance to learn how to have healthy, loving relationships with others, they often turn to a compulsion, in this case food, to fill the emptiness and loneliness in their lives.

Confusion

"I don't like boys to pay too much attention to me. It makes me feel uncomfortable! When I was thin, boys used to look at me and make embarrassing comments. Now that I have gained weight they leave me alone, but I have stopped doing a lot of the things I used to do,

like playing sports and going to school dances. I won't swim at the town pool because everybody would laugh at me in my bathing suit. I would rather hang out at home and watch television anyway. Who needs all that stuff?"

Growing up isn't easy. Teens must learn to be responsible for themselves and their actions. Sexuality is one of the toughest issues most teens face. Being sexually attracted to other people is both exciting and scary. Some compulsive eaters use food abuse and weight gain to protect themselves from feelings that are new and difficult to understand. Weight gain is often an excuse for compulsive eaters to avoid developing relationships that might lead to sexual feelings and situations.

Fear

Jessica wanted to join the drama club, but she was afraid that everyone would make fun of her and tell her that she was not attractive enough to be on stage. She almost went to audition after school, but then she chickened out. Instead, she went home and ate a whole pizza.

Compulsive eaters may also use their weight to avoid other challenges when they're afraid of failure. Instead of participating in activities that will help them meet new people, or trying new things that will help them learn about life, they convince themselves that they never had any chance of being successful or accepted because they are fat. They turn to food to calm their fears. Food can't judge them or tell them they aren't good enough.

Anger

"Sometimes I get so mad at my mom, I don't know what to do with myself. She's always on my case about something. I'm either not getting good enough grades or I need to dress a certain way or she doesn't like my friends. I can't talk to her because she just doesn't get it! So I sit in my room and eat and eat until I can't feel anything anymore."

Let's take a closer look at anger. Anger surfaces to protect us from feeling vulnerable. When you're feeling angry, it's usually because you're either frustrated by not getting something you wanted, fearful of losing something valuable, or hurt that you have already lost something valuable. That something of value can be another person, or it can be your self-esteem. The fear of "losing face" can make a lot of people angry.

Instead of eating, which helps you to avoid dealing with the primary emotions or the anger itself, you can find safe ways to examine your anger and to do something about it. You might start by writing down what is making you angry. Chances are you won't know at first, so write whatever comes into your head. When you hit on what's making you angry, your gut-level response will tell you that you're right. You will probably feel a flash of recognition. Dealing with angry feelings can be as simple as:

⊙ Clarifying the problem and identifying the source of your anger

⊙ Unmasking the primary emotion beneath the anger

⊙   Dealing directly with the person or
the situation making you angry

⊙   Describing the problem behavior
and explaining how it affects you

⊙   Listening to the other side

⊙   Working together toward a solution

If you are too angry to think straight, grab a pen or sit at the computer and start writing. Exercise or try meditation. Don't stew about what's making you angry. Think through the secondary emotion (anger) and look for the primary emotion. Decide on a course of action. Don't expect to get your way simply because you confronted the person with whom you're angry. He may see things differently. Working toward a solution means taking both of your needs into account. The idea is to change your habit of eating when angry to one of meeting problems head-on.

It's not easy to express anger. There are many people who don't like to have confrontations and will do anything to avoid them. Some people feel that they don't have a right to get angry, or they think that they will lose the important people in their lives if they get angry at them. But anger is a healthy emotion. If it's not expressed, it just builds up inside a person. Some people deal with their anger through compulsive eating. But food doesn't and can't make the anger go away. The anger is still there; it's just buried deeper inside.

Compulsive eaters are inclined to think that they will never find solutions to their problems. However, this is not so. If they learn to make some important changes in attitude and behavior, they can indeed live healthier, happier lives. Many people who have struggled with compulsive eating have recovered and achieved healthy relationships with food. You can, too.

Jealousy

Jolie had had a crush on Brad since the first day of school, and it seemed as if Brad really liked her, too! In history class, where he and Jolie sat next to each other, Brad would always joke and talk with her. Sometimes their conversations would take the form of notes passed back and forth. At other times Brad walked with Jolie to her next class.

Jolie was excited because she had always felt like the ugly duckling. She never wore the most stylish clothes and she was, as her mother always reminded her, "a little on the chubby side." But she was a good student and had a quick sense of humor, and it seemed as though Brad enjoyed her company.

One day in history class the teacher seated a new girl right next to Jolie and Brad. Suddenly Jolie felt invisible. Brad was talking with the new girl the way he used to talk with her. Then he asked the new girl for her phone number! Jolie was crushed. She could barely make it through the rest of the school day. When she got home, she went straight to the refrigerator and peered in.

Ice cream, leftover mashed potatoes, chicken, peanut butter and jelly sandwiches, chocolate milk, tortilla chips and guacamole. Jolie ate and ate. As she ate, she thought to herself: "You don't deserve to be jealous! You're fat and ugly. Why would Brad like you? Are you surprised? Because you shouldn't be. Get used to it!" The harsh voices in her head repeated the insults as she continued to eat. When she stopped eating, she thought to herself: "There! I don't care anymore if Brad likes her and not me. What's the use in being jealous?"

For some people, any strong emotion triggers compulsive eating. If you are one of them, ask yourself why you suddenly feel like eating. If you overeat when you're happy, is it because you're afraid your good feelings won't last? Is it because you don't think you deserve to be happy? You must bring these feelings to the surface before you can begin to make changes in your behavior. If you have trouble making positive changes in your life, you may find that it's because your family is working to keep you from changing. Take the following TRUE/FALSE test to see if your family is a hindrance to your efforts to change.

The more TRUES in your answers, the more likely that your family is resisting your efforts to make some healthy changes. If that's the case, you'll want to find a better support system. Sometimes people need more help than their families can give.

A food diary is one self-help measure that pinpoints the feelings and situations that prompt you to binge. Most likely, you'll find that you binge when you feel that you have no control over a certain situation. Use your food journal or your diary

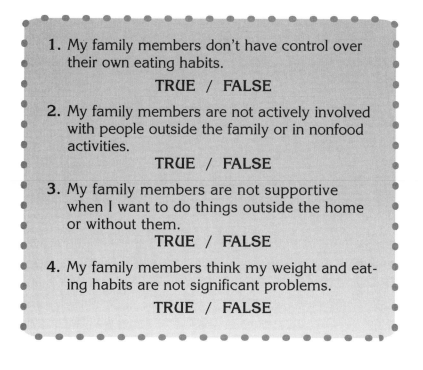

1. My family members don't have control over their own eating habits.

   TRUE / FALSE

2. My family members are not actively involved with people outside the family or in nonfood activities.

   TRUE / FALSE

3. My family members are not supportive when I want to do things outside the home or without them.

   TRUE / FALSE

4. My family members think my weight and eating habits are not significant problems.

   TRUE / FALSE

to discover which feelings push you toward food and which feelings push you away from food. Eventually you will get to the point where you will notice when your feelings are causing the desire to eat. If you deal with your feelings at this stage, you may be able to stop the urge to binge and break the cycle of compulsive behavior.

DEALING WITH STRESS

If you eat when you're anxious, take a look at what kinds of situations make you anxious. Can you do anything about these situations to lessen your anxiety? It's usually the combination of feeling anxious and powerless that sets people up to binge.

Conflict often makes people feel anxious

because most people view conflict negatively and want to be rid of it. Actually, conflict is neither good nor bad; it simply is. If a situation causes you discomfort, you need to meet it head-on. Clarify the problem so that you can then work toward a solution. Some people are afraid to speak up to authority figures such as teachers. Then, believing the problem to be unsolvable, they may go home and eat. It is much healthier to meet with the teacher, discuss the problem, and decide together how to fix things.

If you can't immediately fix a problem, you can still find ways to relieve anxiety. Some people meditate every morning or in times of stress, such as right before a major test. You don't have to chant or repeat a mantra when you meditate; you can simply try to empty your mind and clear away all of your thoughts. Exhale slowly, concentrate on the sounds around you, and tune in to your own breathing. The mind can't hold on to two different feelings at once. You won't remain anxious if you can train yourself to calm down under stress.

Exercising also helps some people to work off their anxiety, and there may be a chemical reason behind this. Hard exercise releases endorphins into the brain and the bloodstream. Endorphins are the body's natural pain relievers. They heighten your sense of well-being while decreasing your awareness of pain. Exercising can be as simple as taking a brisk walk around the neighborhood. Don't think that you have to commit yourself to a rigorous workout every day to manage your anxiety. Compulsive eating can lead to other forms of compulsive behavior, such as compulsive exercising. You don't want to trade one compulsion for another. However, walking, running, playing a hard game of racquetball, or shooting some hoops can be a good way to work off steam. And if the exercise increases your endorphin levels, that's an added bonus.

Finally, it's better to talk out your stress with friends than to go home and eat. You may feel better after sharing your feelings with others, even if the problem doesn't appear solvable. The act of sharing it with someone else decreases the anxiety. The less anxiety, the less the need to binge and purge. Trauma is the one situation that does not easily lend itself to self-help measures. The shock associated with the death of a loved one or some other personal loss may be too great to deal with on your own. If you eat to avoid dealing with the feelings of anxiety or rage that have been stirred up by trauma, you need to seek help from a professional.

DEALING WITH BOREDOM

Some people eat out of loneliness, which may be hard to distinguish from boredom. You may already be sick of hearing your parents nagging you to "paint a picture, read a book, or go for a walk" when you tell them you're bored, but if you find that you are eating to fill up your free time, it might be wise to consider other activities. Keep a list of things that you can do when you're by yourself and bored. Keep your hands busy. If they're doing something, they're not free to reach for snacks.

If you're not sure whether you are feeling bored or lonely, write down a couple of enjoyable things that you could do. Make one of them a solitary activity and one an activity done with another person. Estimate how much you would enjoy this activity, using a scale of 0 (not enjoying it at all) to 100 (having the time of your life). After you have done this exercise, rate how much you really enjoyed each activity. You may discover that you enjoy the solitary activities as much as the ones you do with other people. Therefore, it's not so much that you're lonely, because you can clearly have a good time when you're alone. It's probably more likely that you're bored and have nothing in particular to do.

DEALING WITH NEGATIVE THINKING

If you eat when you are depressed, you may not realize that you can do something more positive about your depression. I encourage my depressed clients to take a good look at the unhappy events in their lives and figure out what they're telling themselves about these events. Bad events don't always get people down; it's what people tell themselves the bad events mean.

Once you can turn your negative thoughts into a more realistic appraisal of the upsetting event, you should find yourself feeling less depressed. You will discover that it's not the event that disturbs you as much as what you think about that event. If you can change your thinking, you will feel less depressed.

Make up a chart with the following headings and keep this chart handy for those moments when you're hit with negative thoughts. Writing those down helps you to see how unrealistic most of them can be.

For example, one person's upsetting event

UPSETTING EVENT	NEGATIVE THOUGHTS	MORE REALISTIC APPRAISAL

might be that her mom is drinking again. Her negative thoughts might be: I will have to manage the household now, and I won't have time for basketball. Then my coach will throw me off the team, and I will never get to play for any other team. I will lose my skills and won't get a basketball scholarship to college, so I will probably never get to go to college. These negative thoughts sound very dramatic, but that's often what happens when we let our thoughts run away with us. We don't usually put them down on paper, so we don't realize how exaggerated they sound.

Decide what's wrong with these thoughts, or what you can do to keep these fears from actually happening. In this example, the girl should have realized that her coach wouldn't throw her off the team if she approached him with the problem. Or even if he let her go, she still was a good enough player that someone else might pick her up. In the worst case, she might not be playing basketball and might lose some of her skills, but that doesn't mean she would never get to college. There are other types of scholarships, in addition to grants and loans. The upsetting event—her mom's drinking—wasn't causing her to feel out of control. Her mistaken beliefs were causing her to feel out of control. If she realistically confronted her fears, she would feel more in control.

Again, it will help to write down the upsetting event. Then record your negative thoughts about that event. You have to be able to distinguish between the upsetting events and the negative thoughts you are having. The solution lies in attacking the negative thoughts, because the thoughts are the problem more than the event is. You can always change your thoughts, even if you can't necessarily change the event. If you have done this exercise, but still feel a need to eat, that's okay for now. Recognizing the thoughts that trigger your binges is a big step in the right direction, even if you are not yet able to refrain from overeating, or bingeing and purging. As you become more aware of your triggers, try to avoid them altogether. Here are some other points to keep in mind.

1. Eat more slowly. Eating should not be a race.

2. Chew your food thoroughly. Chewing everything at least twenty times will force you to slow down.

3. Stop eating when you sense that you are no longer hungry. That means leaving some food on your plate if you sense that you are full. If you force yourself to eat until you are stuffed, you lose the ability to sense the physical discomfort of being full, and you will grow accustomed to that discomfort.

If you eat to reward yourself, find other ways besides food to treat yourself. Take a nice bubble bath, call a friend long-distance, buy an inexpensive book you have been wanting to read. The idea here is to break the connection between food and a reward. If your family celebrates with food, introduce other activities in its place. Maybe they celebrate with food because that's what they have always done. Give them some other options; for example, make games a part of family activities.

Finally, if you nibble a lot during the day, keep your hands busy. Think about your hunger chart and don't eat if you're not really hungry. If you can't refrain from sampling food while you cook, try eating a sour pickle first. The taste will discourage you from eating something sweet. If you don't have any sour pickles handy, go brush your teeth. Clean, fresh teeth and the minty taste of toothpaste may discourage you from eating.

Most important of all, don't be hard on yourself. Do the best you can to make sense of your eating habits, and if you slip up, consider yourself human and go on from there. If you are an emotional eater, you will be tempted to soothe yourself with food once you slip up, and then you will condemn yourself. Recognize this tendency in yourself, and your slips will be fewer. You will learn from your mistakes.

DEVELOPING A HEALTHY ATTITUDE TOWARD FOOD

Working to develop a healthy relationship with food and a positive self-image are two very important aspects of your life. These are not easy things to do, however. Even after we recognize the different influences on our eating habits and self-image, it is still difficult to accept ourselves as we are. This is because we still have to function in a world that sends us mixed messages about food and dangerous messages about body shape and size. But that doesn't mean that we shouldn't try to eat in a healthy way and feel good about ourselves.

In fact, you can make changes now that will benefit you in the future. The choices and decisions that you make today can give you a foundation for facing the many challenges in the years to come. Accepting yourself and learning to appreciate all the individual qualities that make you a unique person will give you the strength and confidence you need to excel in all aspects of your life.

Glossary

addiction   An obsessive and uncontrollable need to use a certain substance or practice a certain behavior.

amenorrhea   The absence of the monthly period in a woman who is not pregnant.

anorexia nervosa   An eating disorder in which one intentionally starves oneself.

antidepressant   A drug to relieve or prevent depression.

binge   To consume large amounts of food, often in secret and usually uncontrollably.

bulimia nervosa   An eating disorder in which one eats large amounts of food and then rids the body of the food by either forcing oneself to vomit, abusing laxatives or diuretics, taking enemas, or exercising obsessively.

calorie   A unit to measure the energy-producing value of food.

compulsive eating   An eating disorder marked by the uncontrollable eating of large amounts of food.

dehydration   The loss of an excessive amount of water or body fluids.

denial   Refusal to admit the truth or face the reality of a situation.

depression   A feeling of sadness that lasts a long time and needs to be treated with the help of therapy or medication.

deprive   To withhold something or take something away.

diuretic   A drug that causes an increase in the amount of urine the kidneys produce.

electrolyte imbalance   A serious condition in which a person doesn't have enough of the minerals necessary for a healthy body.

esophagus   The tube through which food passes from the throat to the stomach.

estrogen   A female hormone.

fasting   Going for a period of time without eating any food.

genetic   Relating to how people inherit traits and appearances from their parents.

indulgent   Giving in easily to wants and desires.

inpatient   A patient who remains in a hospital or a clinic for treatment.

internalize   To bottle up problems or emotions.

laxative   A substance that brings on a bowel movement.

menstrual cycle   A monthly cycle experienced by women that includes the making of hormones, the thickening of the uterine lining, the shedding of the uterine lining, and menstruation (bleeding).

nutrients   The proteins, minerals, and vitamins a person needs to live and grow.

obsessive   Determined to the point of being unreasonable.

osteoporosis   A condition in which the bones become fragile.

outpatient   A patient who does not live in the hospital but who visits on a regular basis for treatment.

overachiever   A person who strives for success beyond what is expected.

psychiatrist   A doctor who is trained to treat people with mental, emotional, or behavioral disorders.

psychological   Having to do with the mind.

puberty   The time when your body becomes sexually mature.

purge   To clear the body of food, usually through vomiting, exercise, or laxatives.

self-esteem   Confidence or satisfaction in oneself; self-respect.

yo-yo dieting   A habit of losing weight by dieting, followed by regaining weight and the frequent repetition of this pattern.

Where to Go for Help

IN THE UNITED STATES

American Anorexia/Bulimia Association
165 West 46th Street, Suite 1108
New York, NY 10036
(212) 575-6200
Web site: http://members.aol.com/AMANBU

American Dietetic Association
216 West Jackson Boulevard, Suite 805
Chicago, IL 60606
(312) 899-0040
Nutrition hotline: (800) 366-1655
Web site: http://www.eatright.org

Anorexia Nervosa and Related Eating
    Disorders, Inc. (ANRED)
P.O. Box 5102
Eugene, OR 97405
(541) 344-1144
Web site: http://www.anred.com.

Eating Disorders Awareness and Prevention, Inc. (EDAP)
603 Stewart Street, #803
Seattle, WA 98101
(206) 382-3587
Web site: http://members.aol.com/edapinc

Gürze Books
P.O. Box 2238
Carlsbad, CA 92018-9883
(800) 756-7533
Web site: http://www.gurze.com

Helping to End Eating Disorders (HEED)
Brookdale University Hospital
9620 Church Avenue
Brooklyn, NY 11212
(718) 240-6451
Web site: http://www.eatingdis.com

National Association of Anorexia Nervosa and Associated Disorders (ANAD)
Box 7
Highland Park, IL 60035
(847) 831-3438
Web site: http://www.members.aol.com/anad20/index.html

National Eating Disorders Organization (NEDO)
6655 South Yale Avenue
Tulsa, OK 74136
(918) 481-4044
Web site: http://www.laureate.com

Overeaters Anonymous Headquarters
P.O. Box 44020
Rio Rancho, NM 87174-4020
(505) 891-2664
Web site: http://www.overeatersanonymous.org

IN CANADA

Anorexia Nervosa and Associated Disorders (ANAD)
109–2040 West 12th Avenue
Vancouver, BC V6J 2G2
(604) 739-2070

Anorexia Nervosa & Bulimia Association (ANAB)
767 Bayridge Drive
P.O. Box 20058
Kingston, ON K7P 1C0
Web site: http://www.ams.queensu.ca/anab

The National Eating Disorder Information Centre (NEDIC)
200 Elizabeth Street
College Wing, 1st Floor, Room 211
Toronto, ON M5G 2C4
(416) 340-4156

HOTLINES

The Eating Disorder Connection
(900) 737-4044
This is a twenty-four-hour nationwide 900 line

that handles calls for referrals, information requests, and crises.

National Food Addiction Hotline
(800) USA-0088

WEB SITES

The Body Shop
http://www.the-body-shop.com
A Web site dedicated to improving the self-esteem of all people.

Go, girl! Magazine
http://www.gogirlmag.com
An on-line fitness magazine full of positive information and images for young women.

gURL
http://www.gurl.com
An on-line 'zine for young women with good, straight talk about body image.

Something-Fishy Eating Disorders
http://www.something-fishy.com/ed.htm
A helpful Web site that provides information on all aspects of eating disorders.

For Further Reading

Berg, Francis. *Afraid to Eat: Children and Teens in Weight Crisis.* Hettinger, ND: Healthy Weight Publishing Network, 1997.

Berry, Joy. *Good Answers to Tough Questions About Weight Problems and Eating Disorders.* Chicago: Children's Press, 1990.

Bode, Janet. *Food Fight: A Guide to Eating Disorders for Preteens and Their Parents.* New York: Simon and Schuster, 1997.

Cooke, Kaz. *Real Gorgeous: The Truth About Body and Beauty.* New York: W.W. Norton, 1996.

Crook, Marion. *Looking Good: Teenagers and Eating Disorders.* Toronto: NC Press, 1992.

Folkers, Gladys, and Jeanne Engelman. *Taking Charge of My Mind and Body: A Girls' Guide to Outsmarting Alcohol, Drugs, Smoking, and Eating Problems.* Minneapolis: Free Spirit Publishing, 1997.

Frissel, Susan, and Paula Harney. *Eating Disorders and Weight Control*. Springfield, NJ: Enslow Publishers, 1998.

Hall, Lindsey, and Leigh Cohn. *Bulimia: A Guide to Recovery*. Carlsbad, CA: Gürze Books, 1986.

Hornbacher, Marya. *Wasted: A Memoir of Anorexia and Bulimia*. New York: HarperCollins, 1998.

Jukes, Mavis. *It's a Girl Thing: How to Stay Healthy, Safe, and in Charge*. New York: Knopf, 1996.

Kano, Susan. *Making Peace with Food*. New York: HarperCollins, 1989.

Kolodny, Nancy J. *When Food's a Foe: How You Can Confront and Conquer Your Eating Disorder*. New York: Little, Brown and Company, 1992.

Kubersky, Rachel. *Everything You Need to Know About Eating Disorders*. Rev. ed. New York: Rosen Publishing Group, 1998.

Madaras, Lynda, and Area Madaras. *My Body, My Self for Boys: The "What's Happening to My Body" Workbook for Boys*. New York: Newmarket Press, 1995.

Maloney, Michael, and Rachel Kranz. *Straight Talk About Eating Disorders*. New York: Facts on File, 1991.

Patterson, Charles. *Eating Disorders*. Austin, TX: Steck-Vaughn Co., 1995.

Roth, Geneen. *Breaking Free from Compulsive Eating*. New York: Plume Books, 1993.

Sacker, Ira, and Marc A. Zimmer. *Dying to Be Thin: Understanding and Defeating Anorexia Nervosa and Bulimia*. New York: Warner Books, 1987.

Siegel, Michele, Judith Brisman, and Margot Weinshel. *Surviving an Eating Disorder: New Perspectives and Strategies for Family and Friends*. New York: HarperCollins, 1997.

The following books can be ordered directly from Gürze Books, P.O. Box 2238, Carlsbad, CA 92018-9883; (800) 756-7533. They will be sent in a plain, unmarked package.

Cohen, Mary Anne. *French Toast for Breakfast: Declaring Peace with Emotional Eating*.

Hall, Lindsey, ed. *Full Lives: Women Who Have Freed Themselves from Obsession with Food and Weight*.

Zerbe, Kathryn. *The Body Betrayed: A Deeper Understanding of Women, Eating Disorders, and Treatment*.

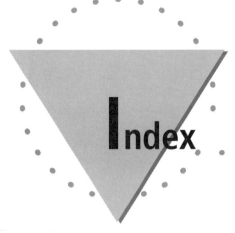

Index

A

alcohol abuse/addiction, 2, 24, 30, 35, 54, 76
anger, 26, 27, 39, 40, 85, 96, 98–100
anorexia, 2, 4, 5–7, 10, 11, 13
Anorexia Nervosa and Related Eating Disorders, Inc., (ANRED), 12
anxiety, 39, 40, 96, 103–105
athletes, 2, 12

B

binge eating, 28–30, 31–33, 34, 41, 60, 62, 67, 70, 77, 81, 84, 96, 103, 108
body fat, 20
body image, 11
boredom, 39, 105–106
bulimia, 2, 4, 7–11, 13, 31, 88, 89–90

C

calcium, 49–50, 70
candida, 52
carbohydrate craving, 56, 57
chemical imbalances, 67
clinical psychiatric nurses, 79
comfort eaters, 34
commercials, 4
compulsive exercise, 6, 11–12
conflict, 39, 103
confusion, 97–98
control, 7, 41, 82, 90
counseling, 75, 78
counselors, 2, 75, 76, 77, 80

D

dehydration, 8, 71
depression, 2, 13, 35, 39, 57, 81, 96, 106
diabetes, 68, 69, 71
Diagnostic and Statistical Manual of Mental Disorders, 10
dieting, 3, 7, 34, 35, 60, 64–67
dietitians, 75
diet pills, 18, 65
diuretics, 64
doctors, 2, 3, 49, 53, 67

dopamine, 57
drug abuse/addiction, 1,
    24, 54, 76

E

emotional hunger, 37, 40
endorphins, 57, 104
exercise, 19, 22, 104

F

fad diets, 18, 66
fear, 39, 98
food diary, 91–92, 103
food sensitivities/allergies,
    52–53

G

genetics, 18–19
grazing, 27–28
guilt, 3, 4, 26, 35

H

hunger, 62
hypoglycemia, 50–51, 56,
    68–69, 71

L

laxatives, 87
loneliness, 96–97
love, 27, 40, 45–47, 74, 97

M

magazines, 16
medication, 49, 51, 52,
    58–60
metabolism, 18. 20
Monroe, Marilyn, 17

N

norepinephrine, 57, 59
nutrition/nutritional habits,
    2, 4, 6, 49
nutritionists, 3, 49, 51, 53,
    54, 57, 67

O

obesity, 33, 71, 72
Overeaters Anonymous,
    55, 82–84

P

peer pressure, 18
physical hunger, 37, 40
pleasure, 3., 4
pressure, 1, 3, 35, 48
psychiatrists, 49, 78
psychologists, 49, 78
puberty, 18
purging, 8, 9, 33, 41, 67,
    70, 77, 81, 84, 87,
    108

S

secretive snacking, 25–27
self-esteem, 12, 13, 35, 40,
    73, 90, 94, 99
self-image, 17, 73
serotonin, 56–59
sexual abuse, 2, 40, 41, 77
shame, 3, 13, 26, 35, 74
stored energy, 20
stress, 103–105
subclinical eating disorder, 3
sugar, 4, 49, 50–51, 52,
    56, 61
support groups, 65, 75–76,
    82

T

therapists, 75, 76, 78–80,
    90
therapy, 76–77, 82
triggers, 14, 39, 60, 92–93,
    102, 108

Y

yo-yo dieters, 35